P9-CLO-693

WITHDRAWN

SOCIAL PROBLEMS AND SOCIAL POLICY:
The American Experience

This is a volume in the Arno Press Series

SOCIAL PROBLEMS
AND
SOCIAL POLICY:
The American Experience

Advisory Editor
Gerald N. Grob

Editorial Board
Clarke A. Chambers
Blanche D. Coll
Walter I. Trattner

*See last pages of this volume
for a complete list of titles.*

THE NARCOTIC DRUG
PROBLEM

BY

ERNEST S. BISHOP

WITHDRAWN

ARNO PRESS

A New York Times Company

New York — 1976

Editorial Supervision: SHEILA MEHLMAN

———◆———

Reprint Edition 1976 by Arno Press Inc.

Reprinted from a copy in
The University of Pennsylvania Library

SOCIAL PROBLEMS AND SOCIAL POLICY: The American Experience
ISBN for complete set: 0-405-07474-3
See last pages of this volume for titles.

Manufactured in the United States of America

———◆———

Library of Congress Cataloging in Publication Data

Bishop, Ernest Simons, 1876-1927.
    The narcotic drug problem.

    (Social problems and social policy--the American
experience)
    Reprint of the ed. published by Macmillan, New York.
    Bibliography: p.
    1. Narcotic habit. I. Title. II. Series.
RC566.B49 1976   362.2'93   75-17204
ISBN 0-405-07476-X

THE NARCOTIC DRUG
PROBLEM

30800

THE MACMILLAN COMPANY
NEW YORK · BOSTON · CHICAGO · DALLAS
ATLANTA · SAN FRANCISCO

MACMILLAN & CO., LIMITED
LONDON · BOMBAY · CALCUTTA
MELBOURNE

THE MACMILLAN CO. OF CANADA, LTD.
TORONTO

30800

THE NARCOTIC DRUG PROBLEM

BY

ERNEST S. BISHOP, M.D., F.A.C.P.

Clinical Professor of Medicine, New York Polyclinic Medical School;
Member Narcotic Committee, Conference of Judges and Justices
of New York State; Committee on Habit Forming Drugs,
Section on Food and Drugs, American Public
Health Association.
Formerly Resident Physician, Alcoholic, Narcotic and Prison Service,
Bellevue Hospital; Formerly Visiting Physician and President of
the Medical Board, Workhouse Hospital, New York Department
of Corrections; Fellow Academy of Medicine, Visiting
Physician St. Joseph Tuberculosis Hospital, Con-
sulting Physician to St. Mark's Hospital,
etc., etc.

New York
THE MACMILLAN COMPANY
1920

All rights reserved

COPYRIGHT, 1920

BY THE MACMILLAN COMPANY

Set up and electrotyped.   Published January, 1920.

362.293
B622n

TO
MY WIFE,

WHO HAS SHARED MY BURDENS AND HELPED IN MY WORK, AND WHOSE INTEREST IN AND SYMPATHY WITH MY WORK HAS MADE MUCH OF IT POSSIBLE, THIS BOOK IS INSCRIBED.

PREFACE

This book has been prepared in response to a growing demand that the author group together under one cover some of the material collected out of a varied experience with many aspects and phases of narcotic drug addiction, and with activities in the attempted solution of its problems.

Some of this experience has been previously presented in many addresses before scientific and other societies and in articles in the medical press.

The author is not associated with nor interested in any hospital or institution active in the care of these cases for financial return or pecuniary benefit. He is not the exponent or mouthpiece or proponent of any special or specific " remedy " or " treatment " or method of so-called " cure." He has no axe to grind.

He is not a " specialist " in the treatment of narcotic drug addiction. He is a practitioner of diagnostic and clinical medicine, in whose professional work the care of the narcotic addict has constituted much the smaller part of his activities and studies, and that part has been largely carried on without recompense and often at his personal expense.

Some years ago, through hospital affiliations and duties, the writer was brought to face this problem of opiate addiction and after a while saw in it very important and very interesting clinical problems of physical disease and physical reactions upon which he made observations and studies.

Hospital connections and the publishing of various articles have since that time brought him into association with practically all phases and aspects of activity in the consideration and handling of the narcotic drug problem. He has listened to discussions of the subject by promoters; by reformers of various sorts; by those engaged in legislative, judiciary, administrative, custodial, penological, sociological, psychological or psychiatrical, medical and other lines of work, and by narcotic addicts from all classes and types of people and their friends and relatives, etc., in groups, or as individuals.

Two vital elements seem to the author to have received insufficient consideration in the efforts to solve the narcotic drug problem. One of these elements is the sufferings and struggles and problems of the narcotic addict, and the other is the nature of the physical disease with which he is afflicted.

This book is an effort to accomplish two things, first to present the two elements above stated, and second to outline, discuss and correlate various elements and conflicting activities so that each of us can appreciate the relation of his own endeavor to the whole narcotic drug problem, can realize the comparative importance of his own observations, and can cooperate with the others for the benefit of humanity, for the welfare of society and posterity and for the increased health and happiness and economic usefulness of the individual.

CONTENTS

THE NARCOTIC DRUG PROBLEM

CHAPTER I

⌐ IT is a fact becoming more and more obvious that too little study and effort to interpret their physical condition have been given to those unfortunates suffering from narcotic drug addiction.⌐

We have neglected their disease in its origin and subsequent progress and formed our conception of its character from fully developed conditions and spectacular end-results. We have seen some of them during or after our fruitless efforts at treatment, their tortures and poor physical condition overcoming their resolutions, until they plead for and attempted to obtain more of their drug. We have seen others exhausted, starved, with locked-up elimination, toxic from self-made poisons of faulty metabolism, worn with the struggle of concealment and hopeless resistance, and for the time being more or less irresponsible beings, made so, not because of their addiction-disease itself, but because they were hopeless and discouraged and did not know which way to turn for relief.

What literature has appeared on the subject has usually pictured them as weak-minded, deteriorated wretches, mental and moral derelicts, pandering to morbid sensuality; taking a drug to soothe them into supposed dream states and give them languorous delight; held by most of us in dislike and disgust, and regarded as so depraved that their rescue was impossible and they unworthy of its attempt.

1

We have overlooked, ignored or misinterpreted intense physical agony and symptomatology, and regarded failure to abstain from narcotics as evidence of weak will-power or lack of desire to forego supposed morbid pleasure. We have prayed over our addicts, cajoled them, exhorted them, imprisoned them, treated them as insane and made them social outcasts; either refused them admission to our hospitals or turned them out after ineffective treatment with their addiction still fastened to them. To a great extent the above has been their experience and history.

In great numbers they have realized our failure to appreciate their condition and to remedy it, and have after desperate trials of quacks, charlatans and exploited "cures," finally accepted their slavery and by regulation of their drug and life, their addiction unsuspected, maintained a socially and economically normal existence. Some failing in this, perhaps broken and impoverished, their addiction recognized, have become social and economic derelicts and often public charges.

From these last, together with the addicted individuals from the class of the fundamentally unfit, we have painted our addiction picture. Confined and observed by the custodial official and the doctor of the institution of correction and restraint, or concealed as family skeletons in many homes, descriptions of them have given to the narcotic addicts as a whole their popular status — cases of mental and moral disorder due to supposed drug action or habit deterioration, and based upon inherent lack of mental and moral stamina.

It was with the above conception of these addiction conditions that I began my work in the Alcoholic, Narcotic and Prison Service of Bellevue Hospital, attracted to the service not by hope of helping nor by interest in "jags" and "dope fiends" as I then considered them, but by the mass of clinical material available for surgical and medical diagnosis and study which was daily admitted to those wards. When I left the service after sixteen months of day and night observation, with personal oversight and attempt to care for in the neighborhood of a thousand admissions a month, my early and faulty conception of narcotic addicts was replaced by a settled conviction that these cases were primarily medical problems. I realized that these patients were people sick of a definite disease condition, and that until we recognized, understood and treated this condition, and removed the stigma of mental and moral taint from those cases in which it did not exist, we should make little headway towards solution of the problem of addiction.

It is a fact that the narcotic drugs may afford pleasurable sensations to some of those not yet fully addicted to them, and that this effect has been sought by the mentally and morally inferior purely for its enjoyment for the same reasons and in the same spirit that individuals of this type tend to yield themselves to morbid impulses, curiosities, excesses and indulgences. Experience does not teach them intelligence in the management of opiate addiction and they tend to complicate it with cocaine and other indulgence, increasing their irresponsibility and conducing to their earlier self-elimination.

Wide and varied experience, however, hospital and private, with careful analysis of history of development, and consideration of the individual case, demonstrates the fact that a majority of narcotic addicts do not belong to this last described type of individuals. It will be found upon careful examination that they are average individuals in their mental and moral fundamentals. Among them are many men and women of high ideals and worthy accomplishments, whose knowledge of narcotic administration was first gained by " withdrawal " agonies following cessation of medication, who have never experienced pleasure from narcotic drug, are normal mentally and morally, and unquestionably victims of a purely physical affliction.

The neurologist, the alienist, the psychologist, the law-maker, the moralist, the sociologist and the penologist have worked in the field of narcotic addiction in the lines of their special interests, and interpreted in the lights of their special experiences. Each has reported conditions and results as he saw them, and advised remedies in accordance with his understanding. With very few exceptions little has been heard from the domain of clinical medicine and from the internist. It is only here and there that the practitioner of internal medicine has been sufficiently inspired by scientific interest to seriously consider narcotic drug addiction and to make a clinical study of its actual physical manifestations and phenomena.

The idea that narcotic drug addiction should be accorded a basis of weakness of will — neurotic or otherwise, inherent or acquired — and should be classed as a morbid appetite, a vice, a depraved indulgence, a habit, has been generally unquestioned and the prevailing dogma for many years. It is very unfortunate that we have paid so little attention to material facts and have made so little effort to explain constant physical symptomatology on a basis of physical cause, and that there has not been a wider recognition and more general acceptance of scientific work that has been done.

Despite the years of effort that have been devoted to handling the narcotic addict on the basis of inferiority and neurotic tendencies, and of weakness of will and perverted appetite — in spite of exhortation, investigation, law-making and criminal prosecution — in spite of the various specific and special cures and treatments — narcotic addiction has increased and spread in our country until it has become a recognized menace calling forth stringent legislation and desperate attempts at administrative and police control. And though a large amount of money has been spent in custodial care and sociological investigation on the prevailing theories, and in various legislation, much of it necessary and much of it wisely planned, we have made but little progress in the real remedy of conditions.

It is becoming apparent that in spite of all the work which has been done — in spite of all the efforts which have been made — there has been practically no change in the general situation, and there has been no solution of the drug problem.

In analyzing results of efforts and arriving at causes for failure, it seems to me that it is always wise to begin at the beginning, and to ask ourselves whether we have not started out with an entirely erroneous conception of our basic problem. Is it not possible that instead of punishing a supposedly vicious man, instead of restraining and mentally training a supposedly inherent neuropath and psychopath, we should have been treating an actually sick man? Is it not possible that the addict did not want his drug because he enjoyed it but that he wanted it because his body required it? This is not only possible — it is fact — and the whole secret of our failure has been the misconception of our problem based on our lack of understanding of the average narcotic drug addict and his physical conditions.

In my own experience as a medical practitioner I know that non-appreciation of this fact was the cause of my early failures; and I further know that from the beginning of appreciation of this fact dates whatever progress I have made and whatever success I have attained. In my early efforts as Resident Physician to the Alcoholic and Prison Wards of Bellevue Hospital, devoid of previous experience in the treatment of narcotic addiction, directed by my available literature and by the teachings of those in my immediate reach, I followed the accepted methods. I tried the methods of the alienist; I tried the exhortations of the moralist; I tried sudden deprivation of the drug; I tried rapid withdrawal of the drug; I tried slow reduction of the drug; I tried well-known special "treatment." In other words I exhausted the methods of handling narcotic drug addiction of which I knew. My results were, in these early efforts, one or two possible "cures," but as a whole suffering and distress without relief; in a word failure.

The blame I placed not where it belonged — on the shoulders of my medical inefficiency and lack of appreciation and knowledge of the disease I was treating — but upon what I supposed was my patient's lack of co-operation and unwillingness to forego what I supposed to be the joys of his indulgence. In discouragement and despair I held the addict to be a degenerate, a deteriorated wretch, unworthy of help, incurable and hopeless. Strange as it seems to me now, possessing as I did good training in clinical observation and being especially interested in clinical medicine, in calm reliance upon the correctness of the theories I followed, I ignored the presence of obvious disease.

As to the existing opinion that the addict does not want to be cured, and that while under treatment he cannot be trusted and will not co-operate, but will secretly secure and use his drug — I can only quote from my personal experience with these cases. During my early attempts with the commonly known and too frequently routinely followed procedures of sudden deprivation, gradual reduction and special or specific treatment, etc., my patients beginning with the best intentions in the world, often tried to beg, steal or get in any possible way the drug of their addiction. Like others, I placed the blame on their supposed weakness of will and lack of determination to get rid of their malady. Later I realized the fact that the blame rested almost entirely upon the shoulders of my medical inefficiency and my lack of understanding and ability to observe and interpret. The narcotic addict as a rule will co-operate and will suffer if necessary to the limit of his endurance. Demanding co-operation of a

completely developed case of opiate addiction during and
following incompetent withdrawal of the drug is asking
a man to co-operate for an indefinite period in his own
torture. There is a well-defined limit to every one's power
of endurance of suffering.

Abundant evidence of what I have written is easily
found among the many sufferers from the disease of
opiate addiction who have maintained for years a personal, social and economic efficiency — their affliction unknown and unsuspected. These cases are not widely
known but there are a surprising number of them. When
one of them becomes known his success in handling his
condition and its problems is generally attributed to his
being on a rather higher moral and mental plane than his
fellow sufferers and possessed of will-power sufficient to
resist temptation to over-indulge his so-called appetite.
We have not as a rule considered any other explanation
nor sought more at length for the cause of his apparent
immunity to the hypothetical opiate stigmata. It would
have been wiser and more profitable for us to have re-
spectfully listened to his experiences and learned something about his disease.

The facts in such cases are that instead of being men of
unusual stamina and determination, they are simply men
who have used their reasoning ability. They have tried
various methods of cure without success. They have
realized the shortcomings and inadequacy of the usual
understanding and treatment of their condition. Being
average practical men, and making the best of the inevitable, they have made careful and competent study of
their own cases and have achieved sufficient familiarity
with the actions of their opiate upon them and their reactions to the opiate to keep themselves in functional balance and competency and control. The success of these
people is not due to determined moderation in the indulgence of a morbid appetite. It is due to their ability

to discover facts; to their wisdom in the application of common-sense to what they discover; and to rational procedure in the carrying out of conclusions reached through their experiences. They have simply learned to manage their disease so as to avoid complications. When I tried to account for some of the things I saw by questioning these men who had studied and learned upon themselves, I soon obtained a clearer conception of what opiate addiction was.

When we eliminate the distracting and misleading complications, mental and physical, and study the residue of physical symptomatology left, we make some very surprising and striking observations.

We find that we are dealing fundamentally with a definite condition whose disease manifestations are not in any way dependent in their origin upon mental processes, but are absolutely and entirely physical in their production, and character. These symptoms and physical signs are clearly defined, constant, capable of surprisingly accurate estimation, yielding with a sureness almost mathematical in their response to intelligent medication and the recognition and appreciation of causative factors; forming a clean-cut symptom-complex peculiar to opiate addiction. Any one — whether of lowered nervous, mental and moral stamina, or a giant of mental and physical resistance — will, if opiates are administered in continuing doses over a sufficient length of time, develop some form of this symptom-complex. It represents causative factors, and definite conditions which are absolutely and entirely due to changed physical processes which fundamentally underlie all cases of opiate addiction, and which proceed to full development through well-marked stages.

During the past years I have had under my care a number of excellent and competent physicians of unusual mental and nervous balance and control in whom there could be no hint of lack of courage, nor of deficient will-power, nor of lack of desire to be free from their affliction. Possessing, some of them, unusual medical training and scientific ability, having added to this the actual experiences of opiate addiction, they with others have co-operated and aided in experiment, study and analysis, and the result has been in their minds as in mine, complete confirmation of the facts above stated.

Primarily, there are two phrases I should like to see eliminated from the literature of opiate drug addiction. I believe they have worked great injustice to the opiate addict and have played no small part in the making of present conditions. It seems to me that to speak and write as we still often do of " drug habit " and " drug fiends " is placing upon the opiate addict a burden of responsibility which he does not deserve. If long ago we had discarded the word " habit " and substituted the word " disease " I believe we would have saved many people from the hell of narcotic drug addiction. I believe if it had not been for the use of the word " habit " that the medical profession would long ago have recognized and investigated this condition as a disease. A man, physician or layman, believes that he can control a habit when he would fear the development of a disease. Until now, however, the description has been " drug habit." And the man who acquires one of the most terrible diseases to be encountered in the practice of medicine is unconscious of his being threatened with a physical disease process until this process has become so developed and so rooted that it is beyond average human power to resist its physical demands.

In the near future, I earnestly hope the true story and the real facts concerning the opiate drug addict will become universally known. Without familiarity with them and understanding of them, and comprehension and appreciation of their disease, we shall never make real progress in the solution of the narcotic drug problem. From the present day trend of articles and stories in the newspapers and lay and medical magazines it cannot be doubted that the time is not far distant when in the lay press will appear, in plain, sober, unvarnished truth, the true story of the experiences and struggles of the opiate drug addict. I have marked a rapidly growing appreciation of facts and a steadily increasing activity in the investigation of conditions. This is sooner or later bound to be followed by intelligent public and scientific demand for competent and common-sense explanation and solution.

CHAPTER II

My earliest efforts in the handling of narcotic addicts were institutional. They were along the lines of forcible control, based upon the theory that I could expect no help nor co-operation from my patients.

While this theory is undoubtedly true as applied to many of those who have developed opiate addiction, it is true of them as individuals whose personal characteristics are such that they require forcible control for the accomplishment of desirable ends in general. It is not true of them simply because of narcotic addiction. It is equally true of these same people afflicted with other diseases. Their successful handling for tuberculosis, venereal disease, cardiac conditions, or anything else requires for its successful issue constant overnight and what practically amounts to custodial care. I shall refer to them later. They are fundamentally custodial or correctional cases and success in their handling will never be accomplished in any other way, whether they are being treated for narcotic addiction or for anything else, mental, moral or physical.

What appears in this chapter does not solve the problem of the handling of the narcotic addict of this type. There are many factors and elements in their mental and physical make-up other than drug addiction which should be considered, and these factors and elements lie at the bottom of their irresponsibility and the real difficulty of their handling.

Experience and the analysis of unsuccessful effort and results showed that, however necessary forcible control might be in the handling of some narcotic addicts, it was

11

not successful nor sufficient nor. even the most important factor in the treatment of most cases of addiction-disease.

I soon came to see that I had an erroneous conception of my medical and clinical problems and an unjust attitude towards many if not most of my addiction patients. Studying them — not as drug addicts, but as individual human beings — I found them in their personal, mental, moral and other characteristics, as various as people suffering from any other disease condition. There were no narcotic laws at that time and opiates were easily and cheaply obtainable. Very many, perhaps most of those who came to my wards were not forced in either by fear of the law or by scarcity of opiate supply. They did not have to come for treatment, but voluntarily presented themselves in the hope of cure. Something was wrong with my theories.

In seeking for solution I began to realize that the narcotic addict of average individual characteristics obtained no enjoyment from the use of his opiate, and that he co-operated as a rule to the extent of his ability and endurance in efforts to relieve him of his condition, so long as he had any hope of possible ultimate success. I learned, trained and experienced physician though I was, that I was far more ignorant of the clinical manifestations and physical reactions of narcotic drug addiction than many of the patients I was trying to treat. It was soon evident to me, moreover, that the man who recognized my ignorance above all others was my patient. I came to see that what I had interpreted as lack of co-operation was largely due; first to his memory of previous experience, second to recognition of my ignorance, and third to his anticipation of useless and harmful suffering which he expected from my care and treatment of his case.

Looking back over that period, I am free to confess that my efforts, though honestly made, amply realized his expectations.

I began to see that I knew nothing of this disease or how to treat it as a problem of clinical disease. I saw that addict after addict sneezed and trembled, jerked and sweated, vomited and purged, became pallid and collapsed, that his heart and circulation were profoundly and alarmingly disturbed, that he had the unquestionable facies or expression of intense physical suffering, and the many constant and obvious signs which attend physical need for opiate drug. I could not escape the conclusion that here were tangible, material, incontrovertible physical facts for which I had no physical explanation. It seemed unreasonable to be satisfied with any explanation of them that did not have a physical basis; and it seemed a logical conclusion that the establishment of a basis of physical disease mechanism could offer the only hope of remedy. I therefore ignored for the time being my past teachings and ideas of the drug addict, and I looked to the patient himself, questioning him as to his experiences and studying the symptomatology and physical phenomena he presented. In short, I adopted the attitude which must be widely adopted before the medical problem of the clinical handling of drug addiction will be solved — in my attitude towards these cases I became the clinical student and practitioner of internal medicine, treating my patient to the best of my ability as I would a sufferer from any other disease, and studying his case.

Struck by clinical facts which did not accord with past teaching, I tried to seek out from my personal study and observation of the individual case data upon which to form theories which would accord with clinical facts and with verified histories and, if possible, give a basis of help to these unfortunates.

Gradually since then I have gotten together, from my own work and that of others, and with some success attempted to interpret and explain and apply, what seemed to me facts about opiate addiction. To my mind and in my experience these facts offer a beacon-light of hope and assure ultimate rescue to a very large proportion if not most of those suffering from narcotic drug addiction-disease.

It is well to state here that of late some of these facts have secured recognition in medical and lay authoritative announcement and literature. The Preliminary Report of a special investigating committee of the New York State Legislature is quoted from elsewhere in this book, and the report in June, 1919, of a special committee appointed by the Secretary of the Treasury speaks of, " the more or less general acceptance of the old theory that drug addiction is a vice or depraved taste, and not a disease, as held by modern investigators."

It is on account of " the more or less general acceptance of the old theory " that it is necessary in this place to discuss some of the tenets of that theory for the benefit of those whose interests or emergencies have not led them to investigation of and familiarity with the scientific and other writings on this subject of recent years.

It has been demonstrated to be a fact that description of narcotic drug addiction as " habit," " vice," " morbid appetite," etc., absolutely fails to give any competent conception of its true characteristics, and clinical and physical phenomena. A large majority of opiate users are gravely wronged in a wide-spread opinion still prevalent. This opinion, as previously outlined, is that chronic opiate addiction is a morbid habit; a perverted appetite; a vice; that only he who is mentally or morally defective will allow it to get a hold upon him; and that its main and characterizing manifestations are those of mental, physical and moral degeneration. Opiate addicts are supposed to have irrevocably lost their self-respect, their moral natures and their physical stamina. They are still painted by many, as inevitable liars, full of deceit, and absolutely untrustworthy — people who are supposed to use a dream and delight producing drug for the sensuous enjoyment it gives them, and who do not want to discontinue its use.   They are thought of as physical, mental and moral cowards who, after realizing their deplorable condition, refuse to exert " will-power " enough to stop the administration of opiates.

With these views I did my early work on this condition. On these hypotheses, trying to follow current available literature and teaching, I treated my patients for a considerable time with results which superficially interpreted seemed to corroborate both literature and teaching.   Many of them managed to get their drugs even while in the institution, and practically all of them left uncured with but an exceedingly small number of possible exceptions.

From my patients themselves, and from watching and studying them, I later learned the truth, which has since been continually strengthened — that the so-called " discomforts " we think of them as suffering upon withdrawal of their drug, are actually unbearable suffering, accompanied by physical manifestations sufficient to prove this to be so.   I also learned that the supposed delightful sensations which have formed the background of most pictures painted of them, had in many, if not in most of the cases with which I came in contact, never been experienced. If they had ever existed they had long ago been lost and all that remained in opiate effect was support and balance to organic processes necessary to the continuance of life and economic activity.   As I have written, these sensations seem to be, " part of the minor toxic action of the opiate against which the addict is nearly or completely immune and to the securing of which very many and probably a majority of the innocent or accidental addicts have never carried their dosage."   In plain English the sufferer from opiate addiction has, in many if not a majority of cases, never experienced any enjoyment as a result of the drug and has endured indescribable agony in its non-supply.

I do not want to be understood as claiming that opiates will not produce pleasant sensations, nor that they are never used to the end of experiencing these sensations. There is a class of the inherently or otherwise defective or degenerate, who first indulge in opium or its products from a morbid desire for sensuous pleasures, just as they would and do indulge in any form of perversion or gratify any idle curiosity. They are mentally incapable of self-restraint, indulging jaded appetite with new stimuli. They yield themselves to any and all forms of self-indulgence and gratification of appetite. There comes a time when for them opiates, from increasing tolerance and dependence lose power to give pleasurable sensations and become simply a part of their daily sustenance, exacting physical agony as a result of their non-administration. When this occurs they make no effort to control amount or method or use; and overdosage together with conditions incidental to and attendant upon their mode of life soon relieves society of the menace of their membership. As a class they have been regarded as incurable and hopeless — socially, economically and personally unworthy of salvage. To whatever extent this may be true, however, it is not true simply because they happen to have acquired opiate addiction, but because they are fundamentally what they are, diseased, degenerate and defective.

The opiate element is as incidental to their fundamental condition as are the venereal and other diseases from which many if not most of them suffer. Observations and conclusions upon addicts from this type of humanity have been given great prominence in the public press and elsewhere and have had an unwarranted influence in the status of opiate addiction and the conception of and attitude towards the addiction sufferer. Because addicts of this class began to use opium or its derivatives and products to secure sensuous gratification is no reason for stigmatizing the mass of those afflicted with addiction-disease as people of perverted

appetites. No one should study addiction in them unless
he is possessed of sufficient ability in clinical observation
to separate physical signs of opiate addiction from the
manifestations of defective mentality — and unless he has
enough insight and breadth of vision to see behind end-
results, primary causative factors; and unless he has
enough common-sense to refrain from applying to the
worthy many the observations he has made upon the unworthy few.

It is only fair to state in passing, however, that from my
experiences as Visiting Physician in the wards of the
Workhouse Hospital, New York Department of Correction, I am convinced that we all too often casually include
in the above generally considered derelict class of society,
many who under intelligent and humane handling could
be restored to or converted into useful citizens.

There are some above this class, of the type of spoiled
and idle youth, who indulge first in opiates in a spirit of
bravado or curiosity. The tremendous increase in addiction since its spectacular incidental and morbid aspects
became so widely published is largely contributed to from
this class.

There are some who first used opiates to temporarily
boost them over an emergency, post-alcoholic excesses,
severe mental strain, etc.

The majority of narcotic addicts, however, and especially
those developing previous to the activities of the past few
years, present a very different history. Mentally and
morally they are of the same average equipment as other
people. They form a class which might be called " accidental or innocent " addiction-disease sufferers. They had
no voice nor conscious part in the early administration of
opiate, realizing no desire or need for it by name, but
only wishing for the unknown medicine which relieved
their sufferings. Very many addiction patients have received their first knowledge of opiate administration in

the withdrawal symptoms which followed the attempted discontinuance of its use. There is in these sufferers no element of lack of will-power; no trace of desire to indulge appetite or to pander to sensuous gratification. In some, before their condition was recognized, their tolerance for or dependence upon opiate had proceeded to a point where their bodies' demand for morphine was imperative and their withdrawal suffering unendurable. In others, before body need was completely established — with their stamina and nervous resistance below par from sickness and suffering — they have been unable to forego opiate's supportive and sedative and pain-relieving action, or to endure the nervous and other symptoms attendant upon its withdrawal after even a brief period of administration.

As to what the addict is; — the tendency and effect of legislative, administrative, police and penological activities in general have been to place the sufferer from addiction-disease in the position of the criminal and vicious. The tendency of the psychologist and psychiatrist is to analyze him from the viewpoint of mental weakness, defect or degeneration, and to so classify and regard him. The average practitioner of internal medicine, and even the recognized leaders and authorities in this field of medical science will tell you that narcotic drug addiction is a condition to which they have given but little attention and have no clean-cut ideas of its physical disease problems. The addict himself, whose testimony has been all too little consulted or sought, will tell you that he is sick with some kind of a physical condition which causes suffering and incapacity whenever a sufficient amount of narcotic is not administered.

In the above attitudes and statements the administrative, police and penological authorities are right in some cases; — the psychologists and psychiatrists have good basis for their opinions in some cases; — the addict has physical grounds for his statement in all cases — he is always sick, sick with addiction-disease.

In my experience with and study of narcotic drug addiction and the narcotic drug addict, an experience touching practically every phase of the narcotic situation and giving me opportunity to observe the condition in practically every type of individual, the one constant and more and more strikingly emphasized observation has been constant physical symptomatology and the manifestations of pain and suffering and of fear. I have in my possession histories of addicts taken from all walks of life and from all classes and conditions of men. Some of my histories are of patients who were primarily defective, degenerate, weak or vicious. Some of my histories are of people of high mentality; of high ethical and moral standards; of high economic efficiency and social standing. These histories, stripped of names and possibilities of personal recognition, would form a very instructive collection of material for the man, physician, psychologist, sociologist, legislator or administrator who wishes to study the addict as he really is and to get some conception of the diversity of the problems which he presents.

Neglect of this study and absence of this conception is the chief cause of past failure. We have tended to regard and handle and treat and legislate concerning narcotic addicts simply as narcotic addicts, instead of appreciating that different individuals and different types and classes of people who may suffer from addiction-disease present entirely different problems, and require entirely different handling.

If we are going to consider all narcotic addicts as in one class we can with justice only consider those characteristics which are common to all members of that class. There is just one fact and characteristic that stands out as of striking and paramount importance in every one of my histories

— it is the fact of physical suffering upon complete withdrawal of opiate drug, or a supply of that drug which does not meet the requirements of the physical body-need. Whatever or whoever the narcotic addict was before his use of opiate drugs — whatever had been the character and circumstances of the initial administration of narcotic drug — after a time, as I have repeatedly written elsewhere, after addiction-disease has once developed, the history of every opiate addict is that of suffering and of struggle. After addiction-disease is once developed the addict loses whatever euphoric sensation he may possibly have experienced, and all that narcotic administration spells for him is relief from suffering. Without the drug of his addiction he endures intense physical suffering and misery. Without the drug of his addiction he cannot pursue a social, economic, or physically endurable existence. He may have been primarily defective, degenerate, depraved or vicious; his primary administration of the drug may have been deliberate indulgence, disreputable associations, idle curiosity, any combination of conditions which may be stated; — he may have been an upright, honest and intelligent, hard-working, self-supporting, worthy and normal citizen in whom the primary administration of opiate drug was a result of unwise, ignorant or unavoidable medication; — he may have been an ignorant purchaser of advertised patent medicines containing addiction-forming drugs. Whatever his original status, mental, moral, physical or ethical, and whatever the circumstances of his primary indulgence; once addiction-disease has developed in his body the vital fact of his history is the same — subsequent use of opiate drug means not pleasure, not vice, not appetite, not habit — it means relief of physical suffering and the control of physical symptoms.

My present definition of narcotic drug addiction is as follows; a definite physical disease condition, presenting constant and definite physical symptoms and signs, progressing through clean-cut clinical stages of development, explainable by a mechanism of body protection against the action of narcotic toxins, accompanied if unskillfully managed by inhibition of function, autotoxicosis and auto-toxemia, its victims displaying in some cases deteriora-tion and psychoses which are not intrinsic to the disease, but are the result of toxemia, and toxicosis, malnutrition, anxiety, fear and suffering.

To express this somewhat differently — a narcotic drug addict is an individual in whose body the continued ad-ministration of opiate drugs has established a physical re-action, or condition, or mechanism, or process which mani-fests itself in the production of definite and constant symp-toms and signs and peculiar and characteristic phenomena, appearing inevitably upon the deprivation or material les-sening in amount of the narcotic drug, and capable of immediate and complete control only by further adminis-tration of the drug of the patient's addiction.

In plain English, the sufferer from narcotic drug addic-tion-disease is one who experiences the symptoms and signs referred to above and which will be discussed later, as a result of lack of supply or physically insufficient supply of opiate drug. I know of no definition along any other lines which will include all who suffer from narcotic drug addiction. This symptomatology, and the mechan-ism or process which produces it, are the only common and characteristic attributes and possession of all opiate addicts.

How these are developed and how they may be controlled and arrested is the demand which the sufferer from narcotic drug addiction, and society as a whole, are making. Un-til a competent and acceptable answer to this demand is in the general possession of those handling narcotic addic-tion, all other discussions will remain inconclusive, and all other considerations incidental, for purposes of definite and final solution. This is the medical problem of narcotic drug addiction, and until those who handle narcotic addicts, and those who control the handling of narcotic addicts, have recognized it, are familiar with it, and can to some working measure explain and control its sufferings, physical phenomena and symptoms and signs, they are unprepared to assist intelligently and competently in the solution of a problem which now as never before menaces the welfare of society.

CHAPTER III

THE NATURE OF NARCOTIC DRUG ADDICTION-DISEASE

IT is a pertinent question to ask, "What type or class of individuals become narcotic addicts?" The only correct answer unquestionably is, any type or class or individual to whom opiates are given for a sufficiently long time. It has yet to be demonstrated that there is any warm-blooded animal, which following sufficiently prolonged and constant administration of opiate drug, is immune to the development of the symptomatology and constant physical phenomena of addiction-disease.

Color, nationality, social or economic position, age, mental and moral attributes of whatever sort are no bar to the development of the condition. These may influence, of course, the conduct and incidental manifestations of the individual addicted, just as they do in any other condition. The addicted judge, or the addicted physician, or the addicted clergyman, or the addicted man of business or other affairs, or the addicted clerk or industrial worker reacts differently to the sufferings and trials of narcotic drug addiction than does the addict of the underworld, or the heroin "sniffer" of idle and curious adolescence, or the addicted defective, degenerate, or criminal. Also he reacts differently to everything else. What is true of one man who has opiate addiction may be absolutely false of another. One narcotic addict is honest, competent, truthful and intelligent. Another is dishonest, incompetent, untruthful and incapable of appreciation or self-control. Neither the one set of attributes, nor the other, is peculiar to narcotic addicts. They are simply personal attributes

23

possessed by different men and types of men who may or may not be narcotic addicts. If the addict of a higher type displays at times attributes not typical of his pre-addicted days, and seems to show a lowering of his mental and ethical tone, it is well to estimate in his case the influences of past worry, fear, suffering, strain and struggle, the attitude of society, medical and lay, towards him, and the manner in which he has been handled, before blaming it all upon the mere presence and effects of narcotic drug addiction, or of narcotic drug. If such changes were inherent in the action of continued narcotic drug medication, they would be found in all addicts, whereas the fact is that they most decidedly are not.

As to age in addicts there is no limit. I have seen an infant newly-born of an addicted mother, displaying the characteristic physical symptoms, signs and phenomena of body-need for opiate a few hours after birth. This case is discussed more in detail in the transcribed testimony of the New York State Legislative Investigation hearings, (Whitney Committee) pages 1524 to 1529, at which I reported it. The infant undoubtedly developed addiction-disease prenatally, reacting in its unborn body against the presence of opiates, supplied through its mother's blood, exactly, as is now demonstrated through experimental laboratory animals and by clinical study upon adults, this disease is always developed — through physical and constant reaction of the body to the continued presence of opiates, however supplied. There have been many such cases, some of which are matters of medical record. This condition of prenatal development of addiction-disease exists beyond dispute and certainly cannot be explained upon grounds of conscious appetite or deliberate self-indulgence. I am told that there are or until very recently have been old soldiers, veterans of the Civil War, whose addiction dated from medication for wounds received during that struggle. The late Doctor T. D. Crothers told me once that opiate addiction in this country received its first wide dissemination in that way. This points to the serious consideration of what may be an urgent and important medical problem of modern warfare.

This brings us up to the origin of addiction. There is only one actual origin of addiction, and that is the continued administration of an addiction-developing drug sufficiently long to develop the physical manifestations symptomatology, and phenomena and body need for that drug. This statement is the only one which can be made as generally inclusive. I have many records and histories, much correspondence, and other data, collected from addicts, relatives, friends and associates of addicts, physicians, official conferences and workers in the various fields of narcotic endeavor. My material covers an active interest of many years duration, and an experience which has dealt with various types and classes of patients under various conditions. I have held different beliefs at different times, influenced by the demands of my immediate position, and by my best interpretation of my own experience, by the conditions under which I happened to be working and by the class of people coming to my attention under the conditions of my work. At one time I believed that all addicts were defective, irresponsible, degenerated, unreliable and liars, made addicts by curiosity, environment and morbid appetite. At one time I believed that the narcotic addict did not physically need narcotic drug under any circumstances, and that he could get along without it if he only had the will and the desire to do so. I proceeded on that theory for a while in the handling of my cases, and have to thank the illicit supply which is present in all institutions that my mortality was no higher, for it is agreed and on record by many competent authorities that forcible deprivation of opiate drug may at times cause death.

These are examples of a few of the various beliefs and

ideas I have held at various times, and upon which I used to generalize, as is the habit and tendency of those who as yet lack experience or breadth of experience. I have in time found many of my beliefs wholly or partly erroneous, or to apply only to selected groups of cases or to incidental phases and aspects of the main problem. They all have their bearings on the general situation, and may be of primary importance in the immediate handling and control of certain phases of it. I have come now to keep my general statements to the solid rock of basic disease and draw on my past experience for the measure and estimation of associated problems and complications as they arise.

The actual origin of addiction is the administration of opiate drugs continuously over a sufficient length of time. The incidental details in their early administration to those who become addicted vary widely. In the origin of some proportion of addicts, we of the medical profession must sooner or later come to recognize and assume our part, unconscious and innocent, but none the less beyond question. What this proportion is is variously estimated by various authorities and statisticians and investigators. It is now beyond dispute that many cases of addiction-disease had their origin in medication during illness, the condition developing unsuspected by either physician or by patient until its physical manifestations had passed the bounds of control.

The old fallacy that an opiate might be administered safely to a sufferer so long as the patient did not know what was being given him is completely disproven by the evidence of addicted infants, and by the excellent and exhaustive laboratory experiments upon addicted animals by such men as Giofreddi, Hirschlaff and more recently Valenti of Italy whose work, published in 1914, should have widest recognition. This fallacy has been responsible for many a case of addiction. Very many opiate addicts have passed into the stage of fully established addiction-disease before they were aware that they had ever taken an opiate.

Clinical familiarity with the symptoms and signs of beginning and developing addiction should be the posses- sion of every physician and surgeon.   It would save from the physicial sufferings, and mental tortures and fears of narcotic addiction many human beings.   It has been my experience when called in as a medical consultant upon medical and surgical cases whose progress towards recov- ery seems unaccountably tedious and unsatisfactory, to detect as the basis for the lack of function and recuperative power, unsuspected developing opiate addiction in time to prevent its further progress.   Unwisely prolonged opiate medication makes more opiate addicts than we have real- ized.

The addict in whom it is most profitable to study addic- tion origin and development and handling, if we are to get a clean-cut picture of addiction-disease, is the individual who is primarily normal, mentally, morally and physically, whose addiction condition is a result of ignorant, mis- guided or unavoidable medication, either professionally or self-administered.   Their number is far greater than is yet generally appreciated.   Many if not most of them are unsuspected and unknown and they include eminent peo- ple in all walks of life.   They are social, and economic assets whose interests and welfare we cannot ignore when we are considering the disposition and handling of the narcotic addict.

Many of them have gone from one institution to another, and have attempted, in desperate effort to be cured, each newly-discovered and announced specific or theory of treat- ment.   They have never derived any pleasure from nar- cotic use.   For them the narcotic drug has been only neces- sary medication to relieve physical suffering and to main- tain economic existence and the support of themselves and their families.   They should be classed as innocent or accidental addicts — normal and worthy sick people. They earnestly desire treatment and help, and once their addiction process is completely arrested do not tend to return to narcotic drug use. Whatever associations they may have had with the unworthy or unfit of the so-called " underworld " and with illicit and illegitimate traffic has been the result of desperate necessity, in their best judgment, in the obtaining of opiate supply when it has seemed to them to be otherwise denied them, and which was necessary to them for the relief and avoidance of suffering and for the maintaining of a condition making possible self-support and the avoidance of revelation and disgrace.

The narcotic addict of this type presents primarily and fundamentally a purely medical problem. Competent and complete arrest of the physical mechanism of narcotic drug need permanently removes him from the ranks of the narcotic drug user. The problem of his handling is one falling within the province of medical practice. His care is purely and simply a matter of the treatment of disease with medical intelligence and judgment on the established lines of medical practice in disease conditions generally. His after-care is simply such management of convalescence as is needed in ordinary medical cases. The length of his convalescence will depend entirely, just as in other diseases, upon the competency and intelligence of his medical handling and upon his physical condition, reaction, and recuperative ability.

For such a man custodial care and institutional handling under conditions of enforced restraint are undesirable and harmful. His withdrawal from self-supporting citizenship should be for the shortest time commensurate with adequate therapeutic results. He should be restored to normal personal, social, and economic environment and activity at as early a time as possible following his clinical treatment and the arrest of his physical mechanism of addiction-disease. Given intelligent clinical handling, with rational therapeutic treatment, and a comprehensive meeting of the indications of disease in his case, he is no more a subject for unusual restraint and custodial care than is a case of malaria or pneumonia or other medical condition. He is in most cases a clinically curable medical case. He presents the true picture of addiction-disease uncomplicated by the distracting and confusing incidentals often met with in the types of cases more commonly discussed. The development of addiction in a case of this type is a purely physical matter, and is the addiction which should be considered in the fundamental comprehension of basic facts.

Stages of Addiction Development

Every case of well-developed addiction has followed in its development a course through several stages, definitely marked by clinical signs and reaction phenomena. I shall not exhaustively discuss all of these stages and their phenomena. The ones I shall mention will be recognized by most of those who have gone through them or have watched them develop.

1. *Stage of Normal Reaction to Therapeutic and Toxic Doses.*

The manifestations of this state in morphine administration for example are more fully described in our textbooks of materia medica than I can take space for in this book, and are familiar to all physicians. The narcotic and analgesic effect with therapeutic doses; the euphoric and inhibitory action of doses in excess of the therapeutic; the toxic action manifested by the slowed pulse, slowed respiration, and generally arrested metabolism and function are too familiar to need elaboration.

2. *Stage of Increased Tolerance.*

Following continuous and consecutive administration of morphine (and the same is true of other opiates) comes failure to secure the effect which followed the early administration. Larger doses are needed for the relief of pain or other symptoms, or the original doses give relief for a shorter time. Toxic manifestations do not follow what would formerly have been a toxic dose. The patient requires what was formerly a toxic dose to secure the former therapeutic effect. The phenomena of this stage are familiar to every observing clinician who has used or seen morphine used for continued therapeutic action. The patient has acquired an increased tolerance of the drug and a beginning immunity to its toxic action. He does not, however, suffer appreciable hardship from drug deprivation. Discontinuance of the drug causes little or none of the symptoms to be described as " withdrawal signs."

3. *Stage of Beginning Addiction.*

Following the stage of increased tolerance comes a stage where discontinuance or lack of administration of the narcotic drug gives definite signs and symptoms, beginning " withdrawal signs," due to some beginning physical body demand for the drug and completely relievable only by its administration. These signs are identical with the first appearing withdrawal signs in a case of established addiction but as yet do not go beyond the beginning manifestations of " withdrawal " in a completely developed addiction. They are limited to a peculiar nervousness, restlessness, weakness, depression, etc. They persist for a few days only if the drug is denied and are endurable.

As to length of time required for the passage through each of these previous stages or through both of them — dogmatic statement is impossible. The time is apparently influenced by a number of factors. Of course the varying inherent resistance or susceptibility of different individuals to any given disease condition must be considered in this disease. It varies also with different forms of opiates used and their modes of administration. The probable physical factors I am not yet ready to discuss. The recent Report of the Special Committee of the Treasury Department says, " Any one repeatedly taking a narcotic drug over a period of 30 days, in the case of a very susceptible individual for 10 days, is in grave danger of becoming an addict." Certainly a physician should look for the signs and symptoms of tolerance and beginning addiction throughout his opiate administration. It is also well to exhaustively inquire into possible past history of unrecognized addiction in any of its three general stages. Some of those patients who have demonstrated an apparent unusual susceptibility and very rapid development will be found on careful analysis to have experienced an unrecognized or forgotten addiction in some stage of development. I have interesting data on this point.

4. *Stage of Established Addiction.*

In this stage the " withdrawal " symptoms and signs become more evident as results of opiate deprivation. They proceed through the mild discomfort and nervousness of the previous stage to the definite manifestations and constant unmistakable withdrawal phenomena to be described. The patient endures physical suffering and displays all the clinical evidence of it. There can be no question of will-power in this stage, nor of desire for narcotic drug for any other purpose than to escape physical suffering. Whether the patient was primarily an innocent and unconscious recipient of the drug, or of the class of the vicious and weak, he is now fundamentally a sick man, afflicted with a physical disease. Whether or not he ever experienced any euphoria or sensuous enjoyment, he now gets nothing of pleasure from narcotic administration. He gets, *simply,* relief from suffering. The opiate drug has become his *only* immediate means of securing and maintaining a physical efficiency, a semblance of normality. No other drug will take its place. He can take tremendous doses without toxic effect. In this stage, if the drug is denied or withdrawn without competent handling, his suffering and incompetency is not, as in the previous stage, a matter of days but may persist for weeks or months after no narcotic has been administered.

The general stages of addiction-disease development as above rather superficially outlined are not of course sharply marked in their transitions. They slowly merge one into the next and taken together constitute a gradual development from normal reaction to opiate to established addiction-disease.

Most patients are in or nearing the stage of developed addiction when they are recognized or come for treatment. Developed addiction for narcotic drug means physical, bodily need for that drug; functional incompetency and suffering without that drug; comparative normality and efficiency only to be immediately secured and maintained by the continued use of that drug.

This is the situation of the sufferer from addiction-disease until such time as the activity of his addiction-disease mechanism is arrested.

Before I attempt exposition of the mechanism which seems to me best to explain addiction-disease and offer a basis for its rational handling, I shall offer several observations bearing upon physical or body reaction in the state of addiction.

1. Experience of addicts and observations upon them show that the length of time over which an addiction sufferer is free from his " withdrawal " manifestations is in proportion to the amount he has recently taken.

Under conditions eliminating various factors, outside of the addiction mechanism, which may influence this general rule, the ratio between the amount of recent dosage and the interval of freedom is almost mathematical. For example, if under given conditions one grain of morphine will keep an addict free from withdrawal manifestations for four hours, two grains will do this for nearly eight hours and three will have the same effect for about eleven hours. It would almost seem as if there were some substance produced in definite amount in each individual case at a given time, and neutralized or opposed by or in some way negatived in its action by a definite amount of opiate drug.

2. Each addict shows a definite and approximately measurable daily minimum need for the drug of his addiction. If he is suffering from the deprivation of his drug, he will require a certain dose, measurable by its effect upon his symptomatology, before he is made physically comfortable and physically efficient again.

3. The narcotic drug administered to an addict suffering withdrawal phenomena and symptomatology will relieve those manifestations exactly in proportion to the amounts of drug administered. Each addict has a constant sequence of symptoms attending the so-called " dying-out " of the drug. These symptoms are relieved in constant reverse sequence by the administration of the drug, and in exact proportion to the amount of drug administered, various incidental influences being eliminated. A small amount of the opiate will relieve the symptoms last appearing; another insufficient amount will relieve another proportion of the withdrawal signs, and so on, until the opiate drug administered balances in amount the extent of the addict's deprivation, or physical need.

This is almost mathematical in its working, and the average intelligent addict, after a few trials, can tell within a very close margin just how much opiate, in his accustomed form, has been administered by the extent to which it relieves his withdrawal signs. It almost seems as if the narcotic drug acted as some sort of an antidote for some poison present in definite amounts in the addict's body.

CHAPTER IV

I HAVE in previous chapters referred to what are known as "withdrawal signs." By this term has come to be known the manifestations displayed by a sufferer from addiction-disease at such times as his opiate is taken away or "withdrawn," either totally or in part to such an extent that its amount does not meet the requirements of his physical needs.

In observing opiate addicts over a length of time no one can escape the recognition of a chain of constantly present physical manifestations inevitably following the non-administration of the drug of addiction. These may vary in priority of onset, in sequence, and in relative violence of manifestation in different cases, but they are the inevitable result of non-administration of opiate to an opiate addict. I described them as follows in a paper on "Narcotic Addiction — A Systemic Disease Condition," which was published in the *Journal of the American Medical Association,* February 8, 1913. "In a general way they may be said to begin with a vague uneasiness and restlessness and sense of depression; followed by yawning, sneezing, excessive mucous secretion, sweating, nausea, uncontrolled vomiting and purging, twitching and jerking, intense cramps and pains, abdominal distress, marked circulatory and cardiac insufficiency and irregularity, pulse going from extremes of slowness to extremes of rapidity with loss of tone, facies drawn and haggard, pallor deepening to greyness, exhaustion, collapse, and in some cases death."

These manifestations have been noted in various ways and to various extents and have been casually commented upon by most writers of the past. The conception of drug addiction as a " habit " has, however, in the past so overwhelmingly dominated the attitude of writers both medical and lay, that consideration of withdrawal signs as physical phenomena, and the analysis of their origin and mechanism on the basis of physical disease and constant body reaction has received all too little attention. The tendency has been to casually regard or belittle them as a part of the essential picture of narcotic addiction, and to place overwhelming emphasis upon mental desire as an explanation of the drug addict's inability to discontinue the administration of opiate drugs. That these physical manifestations have had such incidental place and consideration in the general handling of the narcotic addict and in the consideration of the drug problem is to my mind the basic cause for past failure. Non-appreciation of them unquestionably explains in part the almost uniform lack of success which attended my own earliest efforts.

One of the obstacles to an appreciation of narcotic drug addiction-disease has been the casual assumption on the part of the average person, both lay and scientific, that opiate drugs act upon the addict, and that he reacts to them similarly to the actions and reactions in the non-addicted individual. Morphine action, however, as commonly observed following therapeutic administration or in experimentation upon un-addicted animals gives no conception of its manifestations in the man or woman grown tolerant to its use. Many of the actions and reactions of opiate upon the un-addicted are practically lost in the addicted, and absolutely new reactions, unfound in the un-addicted individual, become the dominating factors in the opiate medication of the addict.

To some extent the fallacies connected with the general conception of narcotic addiction have arisen from the mistaken application to addicts of opiate experience, experimental or otherwise, of the non-addicted. In the matter of sensations, for example, supposed to follow opiate administration, and to the enjoyment of which is widely attributed the addict's indulgence — in practically none of the opiate addicts, once tolerance and organic dependence are completely established, do these sensations occur. The immediate effect of opiate to the addict, depending upon the extent of tolerance, and the reaction of the patient, in dosage not too much in excess of physical body need, is apparently support to function, the restoration or maintaining of normal circulation and nerve and glandular balance, prevention or relief of the agonizing withdrawal pains and manifestations and of impending collapse.

Opiate is used by the large majority of opiate addicts simply and solely for its supportive action, and a certain amount for each addict becomes as much of a definite need and a necessary and integral part of his daily sustenance as food or air. The dream states and other sensuous results, occasionally observed, are when they occur as part of the minor toxic action of the drug, against which the developed addict is nearly or completely immune, and to the experiencing of which very few of the honest, innocent or accidental addicts have ever carried their dosage. They are commonly found only in the opium pipe smokers, an entirely different problem from that of the average narcotic addict.

As has been stated, it is a fact that for each addict, a definite amount, varying with his condition of health, elimination, physical and mental activity, etc., meets a definite body-need. On this amount he can be put and kept in good physical and mental condition under normal circumstances of environment, exertion, and general hygiene. Years of efficient activity and upright responsible lives, accomplished by well-known men and women, unsuspected addicts, bear witness to this fact. An addict neither underdosed nor overdosed practically defies detection. Less than the definite amount required for nervous and glandular and circulatory support and organic balance deprives the patient of reaction, places his vitality and energy far below par and for a long time hinders his betterment. More than this amount displays the inhibitory effects of opiates, locks up or slows secretions and body functions, and causes malnutrition, autotoxemia, autotoxicosis, and the consequent mental and physical deterioration commonly and erroneously attributed to the direct action of opiate drug.

In 1912 I wrote that so far as I knew the symptomatology attending insufficient supply of morphine (or other opiate) to an opiate addict had never received the amount of detailed study and analysis that it deserved and was not adequately interpreted. W. Marme had attributed the symptoms of morphine addiction to the toxic action of oxydimorphine. Rudolph Kobert, however, stated that Ludwig Toth subjected Marme's claims to subsequent testing and was unable to confirm them, and that his own findings agreed with those of Toth. They found that oxydimorphine was inert by subcutaneous injection and that when thrown into the blood-stream it formed an insoluble substance causing emboli, and so producing the symptoms observed by Marme. Kobert seems to be in accord with the early findings of Magendie, that oxydimorphine is non-toxic. The experiments of Faust on dogs concerning increased power of the body to destroy morphine are well-known. It is still a matter of scientific dispute as to what extent the body of the opiate addict has developed the power to limit or destroy the poisonous properties of opiates by the conversion of these poisons through oxidation or other chemical action.

The explanation of tolerance and withdrawal phenomena on the basis of something akin to an antitoxin or antitoxic substance circulating in the blood of the addict, has also, like the oxidation explanation, been a subject of controversy. Hirschlaff claimed to have produced an antitoxic serum against morphine. Morgenroth failed to confirm Hirschlaff's findings, and argued against the existence of an antitoxin. The animal experimental and laboratory work and findings, however, of such men as Hirschlaff, Giofreddi and Valenti have helped to influence the trend of modern thought towards what may be regarded as the present strong tendency in scientific conception of the physical mechanism of narcotic drug addiction-disease — an autogenous antidotal or antitoxic substance.

A recent paper by DuMez of the United States Public Health Service gives a comprehensive review of the work which has been done in connection with the study of increased tolerance and withdrawal phenomena, and shows conclusively the gradual inclination of modern opinion.

There is considerable literature discussing various theories and experiments and observations, which has, however, not had widespread recognition.

REFERENCES

Bishop, E. S., "Narcotic Addiction — A Systemic Disease Condition," *Journal A. M. A.,* Feb. 8, 1913.

Marme, W., "Untersuchungen zur acuten und chronischen Morphinvergiftung," *Deutch. med. Wchnschr.* 9: 197–198.

Kobert, R., "Lehrbuch der Intoxikationen," Stuttgart, 2; 995, 1906.

Toth, L., "Bemerkungen zur Erklärung der chronischen Morphium Intoxikation," Schmidt's Jahrb. 229: 135, 1891.

Faust, E. S., "Über die Uraschen der Gewöhnung an Morphin" Arch. f exper. Path. u. Pharmakol. 44: 217–238, 1900.

Hirschlaff, L., "Ein Heilserum zur Bekämpfung der Morphinsucht und Ähnlicher Intoxikationen," *Berl. klin. Wchnschr.* 39: 1149–1152 and 1174–1177, 1902.

Gioffredi, C., "L'immunite artificielle par les alcaloides," 28, 402–407, and 31, fasc. 3, 1897.

Valenti, A., "Experimentalle Untersuchungen über den chronischen Morphinismus; Kreislaufstörungen hervorge-rufen durch das Serum morphinistscher Tiere in der Abstinenzperiode," Arch. f. exper. Path u. Pharmakol, 75 : 437–462, 1914.

DuMez, A. G., "Increased Tolerance and Withdrawal Phe-nomena in Chronic Morphinism, A Review of the Lit-erature," *Jour. A. M. A.,* 72 : 1069–1072, 1919.

My own present opinion and conception remains as ex-pressed in a paper, " Narcotic Addiction — A Systemic Disease Condition," written in 1912 and published in the *Journal of the American Medical Association,* Feb. 8, 1913, as follows, " It is my opinion that, however much increased oxidation aids in the handling of morphine, it is to the formation of an antitoxic substance that we must look for explanation of our clinical manifestations and for the classification of morphine-addiction as a definite medical entity.   This opinion is based on certain clinical manifestations of morphine effect and the symptomatology attending insufficient supply of morphine to those addicted, on certain phenomena observed during and following treat-ment, on the persistence of tolerance and on the suscepti-bility of the cured patient to the re-formation of addic-tion."

Before elaborating this conception of addiction-disease, I think it desirable to repeat the enumeration of the prin-cipal manifestations of " withdrawal " or body-need for opiate drug.   In a general way, they may be said to begin with a vague uneasiness and restlessness and sense of de-pression and weakness; followed by yawning, sneezing, sweating, excessive mucous secretion, nausea, uncontroll-able vomiting and purging or diarrhea, twitching and jerking, sometimes violent jactitation, intense muscular cramps and pains (described as if the flesh were being torn from the bones), abdominal pain and distress, marked cardiac and circulatory insufficiency, and irregularity (often with marked dyspnea), pulse going from extremes of slowness to extremes of rapidity, with lowered blood-pressure and loss of tone, facies drawn and haggard, pallor deepening to greyness, exhaustion, collapse and in some cases, death.

Essential Mechanism of Narcotic Drug Addiction-Disease

If such clean-cut, strikingly apparent, constant, and un-deniably physical phenomena and symptomatology as I have described are to be adequately explained, there must be some physical mechanism, some definite body process working upon fundamental principles of disease reaction. They certainly are not psychiatric manifestations nor the expressions of habit, appetite, vice, nor morbid indulgence. Enjoyment of morphine for itself, even in such patients as have ever experienced such enjoyment, is lost long before the stage of rooted or completely developed addiction is reached.   Physical results must be explained by physical cause.

Tolerance of and immunity to the toxic effects of nar-cotic drugs are primary and striking characteristics in the development of addiction.   An antitoxin or antidotal substance is the recognized mechanism of their production in most diseases admittedly developing these characteris-tics.   I have adopted the hypothesis, therefore, that an antidotal substance is manufactured by the body as a pro-tection against the poisonous effects of narcotic drugs con-stantly administered.   Such a substance, manufactured in the body, being antidotal to morphine, might well possess toxic properties of its own, exactly opposite in manifesta-tion to those possessed by morphine and other opiates. Toxic substances exactly opposite to opiate in their action might readily account for the severe withdrawal signs, parallel in their extent to the extent of opiate insufficiency, and resembling in their characteristics the manifestations of acute poisoning.

A hypothetical antidotal toxic substance, manufactured by the body as a protection against the toxic effects of continued administration of an opiate drug, will therefore explain the well-known development of tolerance and immunity in these cases, and will account for the violent physical withdrawal signs. In a word, it will explain the disease fundamentals on a definite physical basis.

Such an hypothesis will explain the stages of development of addiction before outlined. In the stage of tolerance the antidotal toxic substance has begun to make its appearance in the body and to protect it against slight narcotic excess, but its manufacture is not sufficiently established to continue longer than necessary to neutralize the narcotic administered. In the stage of beginning addiction, or beginning narcotic-need, its manufacture has become more developed and more constant and proceeds for a longer time after the discontinuance of the narcotic drug. In the stage of fully developed addiction, or absolute narcotic need, the manufacture of the antidotal toxic substance has become practically an established pseudo-physiological body-process, and will continue long after the administration of the narcotic drug for reasons into which I have gone elsewhere. In other words, in narcotic drug addiction some antidotal toxic substance has become the constantly present poison, and the narcotic drug itself has become simply the antidote demanded for its control In brief, fundamentally and basically, narcotic drug addiction is a condition presenting definite physical phenomena, symptoms, and signs, due to the presence within the body of some autogenous poison requiring narcotic drug for neutralization of it or of its effects.

This explains the phenomena of the mathematical exactness with which the minimum daily need can be estimated under experimental conditions, and with which doses less than the amount of actual body need relieve existing withdrawal signs in definite proportion to the amount of opiate administered. In exact proportion as the drug of addiction is present in the body to neutralize or oppose some antidotal poison, is the patient free from withdrawal symptoms and from physical craving for the narcotic drug.

The development and existence of such mechanism in the body of the opiate addict is suggested also by the apparent continuance of tolerance to opiate existing after long periods without drug in individuals who had previously suffered from addiction-disease, and in the susceptibility of the former sufferer subsequent to the arrest of his physical need for opiate, to the re-establishment of that need by the subsequent administration of the drug.

Illustrative of this phenomenon is a case who, after about two years of relief from addiction-disease, developed pneumonia and to whom in delirium and threatened death, opiates were administered as unavoidable medication. After cessation of his delirium, he was dismayed to discover addiction-manifestations and body-need for opiate drug had been re-established. This history is one of a number in my possession, and has been verified.

The case demonstrating the longest persistence of susceptibility among my records, is that of a man in the early fifties who underwent an emergency operation for infected gall-bladder. A day or two following operation he developed excruciating pain in his right side just under the ribs. It had been necessary to administer opiates since a day or two before the operation. I was called in consultation for the purpose of determining the character and origin of the pain, and diagnosed a pleurisy, the pain of which subsided on the following day. Opiates were discontinued with a result of precipitating unmistakable withdrawal phenomena. To his great anger and surprise, I accused the patient of being an opiate addict. He indignantly declared that he had never used opiates in his life. Subsequent investigation with the aid of older members of his family disclosed a distinct and typical history of addiction manifestations following opiate administration in the course of treatment of a complicated fracture of his thigh in early boyhood. The drug had been withdrawn at that time and the addiction manifestations finally disappeared, he never having been aware of the facts. His reawakened addiction-manifestations were easily and quickly checked.

It is evident from many histories that large dosage robbed of or modified in its toxic effect, and even in the opiate manifestations usual in subjects who have never been made tolerant, and small dosage being sufficient to re-awaken physical need for opiates are conditions which do exist and persist for indefinite periods. The resemblance between this continued tolerance and the conditions existing in diseases which confer immunity and having a generally accepted antitoxin mechanism is too close to be ignored.

Evidence of a toxic substance in the body of a narcotic-addict is further presented by the similarity of the clinical pictures presented by these cases of acute opiate need and extremely severe cases of acute poisoning from materials such as the ptomains and some other poisons. Acute opiate need is clinically typical of intense suffering and prostration from the action of some powerful poison. Its symptoms cannot be due to opiate, for the reason that the administration of opiate relieves them, and relieves them exactly in ratio to the amount of opiate administered. They can be held at any given stage by gradation of the opiate dosage. Their manifestations, moreover, are exactly opposite to opiate effect. They are to my mind best explained as due to the action of some toxic substance, antidotal to opiate, prepared by the body for its protection in response to continued opiate presence in the body, as antitoxins are prepared for the neutralization of or opposition to the organic poisons of invading bacteria. The chemical or physical character or nature of such substance has not been yet determined.

The presence of such a substance would explain the establishing of tolerance, the manifestations following opiate administration and the apparent definiteness of the amount of opiate needed. It would explain the results of under-dosage and the results of over-dosage, and the practical non-interference with function or general health when a dosage is maintained exactly sufficient in amount to neutralize the effect of some exactly antidotal body or substance.

An antidotal substance would also explain the after effects of and the so-called " relapses " which occur after most of the cases treated by whatever method or procedure, without due appreciation and proper estimation of the clinical manifestations and indications of addiction symptoms and physical body need, and without due consideration of the patient's reactive abilities and physical condition. These patients are in a condition of restlessness, discomfort, vague pains, mental and physical depression, lowered physical vitality and weakness. They have a sense of a physical lack of support. They cannot endure nor react to over-exertion, worry, strain, etc. This condition may persist for weeks and months after no opiate has been administered. The above seem to be mild withdrawal symptoms of an incompletely arrested addiction-disease mechanism and might be explained by a continued manufacture of small amounts of antidotal toxic substance, causing a low grade chronic poisoning. They can be duplicated in active opiate addiction before withdrawal by administering an amount of opiate slightly below the amount of need and so leaving unneutralized a small amount of the antidotal toxic substance.

If continued production of a toxic antidotal substance, after discontinuance of the drug which called it into being is to explain the existence of the condition I have just described, the causation of this continued production must be accounted for. It is conceivable that in the development of addiction-disease mechanism a tolerance of and slowness to eliminate opiate or some product of opiate is acquired by all the cells of the body, perhaps especially by the liver, and that these tolerant and atonic cells are extremely slow of opiate elimination. Under this condition, a residue of opiate or some product of opiate capable of antidotal substance stimulation might remain unresponsive, or very slow of response, to ordinary cellular and other elimination. If this should prove to be the fact, it would account for a continued production of antidotal toxic substance, and might, moreover, in any given case, either before or after cessation of opiate medication, be one of the determining factors in the amount of antidotal substance produced, or, in other words, in the measure of the extent of body-need for opiate drug.

Inhibition of Function

What characteristic action exists in opiate or narcotic drugs which gives them this power to establish the above described mechanism? It seems to me that it is, above all, their power to inhibit body function. They tend markedly to arrest metabolic processes. They inhibit glandular activity. They inhibit unstriped muscle activity and hence peristalsis. They, therefore, cause a slowing up of glandular function and intestinal activity, and of elimination. This results in an accumulation of opiate in the body. It is this constant accumulation to which the body must become tolerant by the development of some mechanism for its protection.

Autointoxication and Autotoxicosis

It is to the element of inhibition of function also that we must look for explanation of what is by far the most important element in the immediate picture presented by most individual cases. I refer to autotoxicosis and to auto- and intestinal toxemia. The same power that locks up within the body the opiate drug, locks up the toxic products of tissue activity and tissue waste, of intestinal poisons and of insufficient metabolism. Autotoxemia itself is markedly inhibitory in its action, and contributes no little to its own increase and to the further development of narcotic disease.

It is not at all impossible that any inhibiting poison constantly present in the body will some day be found to establish a mechanism of protection, similar to that of opiate addiction, and that some of the states now popularly and loosely classified under the general head of " autointoxications " will be recognized as really addiction-states, in which the body has become progressively tolerant of its own poisons. I believe that it can be demonstrated that some of the phenomena and manifestations at times observed in chronically inhibited and autotoxic individuals in whom there can be no suspicion of any opiate or narcotic element are analogous to the phenomena of narcotic addiction mechanism. It is not inconceivable that any inhibiting poison or toxin is capable of producing its own addiction-mechanism, and it has seemed to me that my own clinical familiarity with the action and reaction of narcotic, inhibiting, or addiction-forming drugs and of addiction-mechanism upon circulation, glandular and intestinal and other function has been of no little assistance in the interpretation, control and remedy of other chronic intoxications.

Upon the extent of inhibition of function and autointoxication, therefore, depend some of the immediately predominating manifestations in individual cases. They must be reckoned with and eliminated in the measure of addiction-disease in the individual sufferer. In many cases they contribute the immediate and compelling indications for rational therapeutic endeavor. To a considerable extent they determine circulatory efficiency and metabolic and glandular activity and balance. They largely control physical tone and physical reaction. Inhibition and intestinal and autotoxemia cause most of the physical and mental deterioration, and much of the incidental symptomatology so widely ascribed directly to narcotic drug effect. Upon the extent of their presence, therefore, depends greatly the clinical picture in the individual case. This doubtless accounts for the acidosis, noted by Jennings and others, inasmuch as it has been definitely proved that acidosis is commonly present in all conditions of functional depression and exhaustion.

With inhibition and auto and other toxemia eliminated or reduced to a minimum, the patient can go through many years, an apparent normal man, well-nourished, reactive, in good physical tone, mentally sane and physically competent. Under these conditions he shows practically nothing abnormal as long as he gets properly administered, his accustomed narcotic drug, in the amount of its minimum physical requirement or body-need. His condition is often unsuspected by those nearest and dearest to him, and the popularly held opinion that narcotic addiction shortens life does not seem to be upheld by the facts in his case. Such cases as his are far more numerous than has as yet been realized.

In the types of narcotic addicts most widely recognized inhibition of function and autointoxication is marked, and the opiate drug is used in excess of body-need. The addict of this description becomes a deteriorated wreck, requiring high doses of opiate for the satisfaction of abnormal body-need, mentally and physically incompetent — the generally accepted picture of the so-called " dope-fiend," a deteriorated, degenerated, malnourished wretch, degraded, avoided and condemned.

Inhibition of function and autointoxication should not

be vague terms. They cause and are measurable by definite clinical evidence. They display manifest phenomena and symptoms, and become increasingly defined material entities as the clinician looks for them as such. Much of inhibition of function and autointoxication and of their manifestations, has been recognized and taught under their own heading and in connection with conditions other than narcotic drug addiction-disease. That the influence and importance of inhibition of function and autointoxication in the development, and manifestations of the narcotic drug addict has escaped general and widespread recognition, is evidence of the small amount of unbiased clinical study, and of analytical clinical interpretation of material physical phenomena, hitherto accorded to narcotic drug cases.

I would not have it concluded that all symptoms and manifestations arising in the handling of a drug addict are due to the factors and elements I have discussed in this chapter. It must be always in the mind of the intelligent and conscientious physician, that he has in his care a human being with the same medical and psychical possibilities that must be taken into careful and complete account, as in the handling of any other sick person. There is an unfortunate tendency to overlook concurrent, or complicating or pre-existing conditions in the handling of the narcotic drug addict. These cases are often extremely complex and difficult to analyze, and for adequate comprehension and handling of them, the symptoms and manifestations they show should be appreciated in their true origin and character as they occur in each individual case.

CHAPTER V

MOST physicians have at some time or other in the course of their practice encountered cases of narcotic addiction. Most addicts have appealed to the physician for advice and help. A very large proportion of them have at different times made effort to obtain relief from their affliction through the avenues of various forms of treatment, advertised and otherwise. Most physicians have at some time or other made effort to rescue some victim from drug addiction, and as a rule have given over the effort as hopeless, because even when they had succeeded in taking his narcotic away from the patient, usually after an experience trying and exhausting to both, the patient has resumed narcotic administration — according to the patient, because he had to — according to the average observer, because he wanted to. Frequently the patient has refused to persevere to the end of treatment and has abandoned his attempts before the treatment has reached the point of cessation of opiate medication — the patient stating that he could not — the observer believing that he would not, continue, and did not have the courage or stamina or will to endure the necessary suffering. The medical profession as a whole has adopted a cynical attitude towards the possibility of permanent "cure," and towards the efficacy of medical treatment, which has tended to send the addict to quacks and charlatans and various advertised remedies.

It is not my purpose to discuss in this book in detail

the various methods, and treatments and cures advocated and employed in the handling of the drug addict. This alone would require a volume in itself.

Three broad lines of procedure have been employed; so-called "slow-reduction," "sudden withdrawal," and withdrawal accompanied by the administration of various drugs, such as those in the belladonna group and its alkaloids.

Slow reduction or "gradual reduction" as a "method" is employed by slowly or gradually reducing the patient's accustomed dosage to the point of discontinuance of opiate medication. Interpreted by a great many to mean that the fact of reduction is the principal indication in clinical procedure, successful in the hands of a few who have acquired unusual technical skill and clinical ability in the interpretation of addiction manifestations, I believe it to have failed as a method of cure in the hands of the average. Practically every addict has attempted it one or more times. As a method of procedure in some stages and under some conditions of addiction treatment, slow or gradual reduction of dosage has its value. In my opinion, however, all other considerations aside, there are very few who are possessed of sufficient understanding of narcotic addiction and ability in the interpretation of clinical indications, and have the technical skill required to carry it through to a clinically successful culmination. As a method of routine or forcible application it has many serious objections as well as potentialities for damage to the patient. In cases whose opiate intake is in excess of actual physical-need, gradual reduction as often practiced is perfectly easy and unnecessarily slow down to the amount demanded as a minimum by the patient's addiction-disease requirements Then must come withdrawal, nagging, exhausting and protracted, if unskillful reduction is persisted in, and the wrench of actual final withdrawal is nearly as severe from a very small dosage as from a moderate one, other conditions in the case, physical and mental, being equal. Prolonged "withdrawal" without rare technical skill and without unusual and not commonly available environment and conditions of life, means subjecting the patient to the continued strain of persistent self-denial and self-control in the face of continued suffering, discomfort, and physical need and constant desire for their relief. It is my opinion that this experience has in many cases tended to deeply impress upon the mind of the patient so-called "craving" for the drug, and has converted many a case of simple physical addiction-disease into a more or less mental state which may be described as "morphinomania" or "narcomania."

This last observation does not apply to the method of gradual reduction only, but is equally true of protracted suffering under any other procedure in which the individual is cognizant of the existence of means of immediate if only temporary relief.

In the comprehension of this a physician has only to glance back over his professional experience and recall cases of various conditions other than addiction which have come to him, and whose histories present the effect of long protracted suffering and discomfort in the conversion of an average normal, self-supporting human being into a dependent neurasthenic.

The histories given by most narcotic addicts of their efforts to get relieved of addiction, show that following the withdrawal of opiate drug in many if not most instances has come weeks and months of weakness, and discomfort, nervousness, sleeplessness, and pain which have persisted for weeks and months, establishing the basis for the much emphasized "after care," of some investigators.

While so-called "after care" is unquestionably as important as convalescence from any other disease, it is my belief that as understanding of addiction as a clinical disease becomes more general, and more attention is paid to the study and scientific management of the disease itself, the stage of "after care" will come to assume less importance. Addiction is not the only disease which furnishes examples of cases in which incomplete and unsatisfactory results have been merely a low-grade continuation of the fundamental disease and have been interpreted as a protracted convalescence.

"After care," or convalescence, following satisfactory results of clinical treatment and complete arrest of addiction-mechanism activity has no terrors for either physician or patient. It is very short and does not require any more restraint than any other convalescence, unless conditions exist following active treatment which should have been recognized and handled and eliminated earlier from the picture. I shall discuss this again later.

"Sudden" or "forcible" withdrawal, or immediate deprivation of opiate drug is still advocated by some investigators, fewer and fewer of them, however, among medical men. There are cases of, and stages in addiction-disease and its development where this means of procedure may be pursued without all of the serious objections with which it must be regarded as a routine method of general enforcement.

That forcible deprivation of opiate drug may end in death is a matter of too easily found and authoritative medical record to be ignored. It has been discussed as one of the possibilities by medical writers over many years. Even the newspaper reports of deaths and suicides following sudden deprivation of opiate should be sufficient to give pause to those who would still advocate this measure as a desirable procedure.

Reference to the previous enumerations of the physical manifestations of body-need for opiate, or "withdrawal signs," should be sufficient for the comprehension of its tortures and easily explains the suicides which have attended sudden deprivation. Any one who has watched a well-developed case of addiction-disease in the agonies of opiate deprivation should hesitate to prolong them if possibly avoidable. While under some conditions, and in some cases, it may be argued that "the ends will justify any means," as a routine procedure of wide application, it must be stated that both in its immediate torment and in its end results, mere forcible sudden withdrawal is not a procedure of election. Some of its supporters still cling to and quote the old fallacy that after seventy-two hours without opiate a narcotic addict no longer physically requires it. This fallacy is probably based upon the estimated maximum time of opiate elimination in normal human beings and experimental animals. It is most decidedly false doctrine as applied to the well-developed case of addiction-disease in whom the mechanism of disease, and not the mere administration or elimination of opiate has become what should be the dominating consideration.

As stated before, the mere withdrawal of opiate drug does not arrest the activity of addiction-disease, nor prevent the endurance of the exhausting and incapacitating and protracted low-grade manifestations before referred to. Its potentialities of permanent damage, moreover, are attested by and displayed by many who show for years shattered nerves, premature old age, etc.

It is perhaps wise to state again in this place that in this book the consideration of narcotic or opiate addiction, its mechanism symptomatology and handling, is not to be applied to cocaine and alcohol use nor to the various other drugs often loosely grouped with opiates as "habit-forming." Until a distinct physical disease mechanism, attended by analogous characteristic and constant physical phenomena, can be demonstrated as resulting from the action of one of these drugs or substances, its continued use should not be classed with opiate addiction-disease.

The third general method of procedure is that in which

effort is made to utilize other drugs than opiates, or other
measures than mere reduction or withdrawal or deprivation to secure cessation of opiate medication.   The efforts
have been, in a general plan, either to oppose or replace
the action of opiate by substance or substances seemingly
to have physiologically antagonistic or substitution properties — or to combat, offset or benumb the sufferings of
what is described as the " withdrawal period."   Such
agents have been employed in this disease for very many
years, and in their variety include most of the known
analgesic, sedative, antispasmodic, hypnotic or anesthetic
agents and measures.

Prominent among the drugs mentioned have been the
preparations and alkaloids of belladonna, of hyoscyamus,
pilocarpine, and some others.   These drugs have by reason of more or less supposed specific action, alone, or in
various combinations or in conjunction with purgatives,
etc., formed the basis for many if not most of the various
special treatments and " cures."   For example, what is described as the " specific mixture " of one of the most
widely-known treatments contains as its active agents
belladonna and hyoscyamus.   These drugs are not mentioned here in condemnation of their employment as therapeutic measures in the hands of those skilled in the estimation of their values, indications and actions — and
dangers if unskillfully employed.   They have unquestioned therapeutic value in their proper places, as and
when properly indicated, in individual cases.   Routinely
used, as specific curative agents, they seem to me to be
demonstrating their failure.   In the conception of addiction-disease herein outlined it is difficult to attribute to
them specific properties.

In a paper, " The Rational Handling of the Narcotic
Addict " read before the Section on Pharmacology and
Therapeutics, Annual Session of the American Medical
Association, 1916, I stated, " It is not my purpose to en-

ter into discussion of the various therapeutic methods and
therapeutic measures which have been advocated and employed in the treatment of narcotic addiction. Their
number is legion, and they include most of the therapies
known to lay as well as to medical literature.

" Their multitude is conclusive proof of lack of conception and of understanding of addiction-disease in the past.
They have been directed towards incidental and complicating manifestations. They have no more place in
the treatment of the addict than they have in the treatment of any other disease condition. I know of no medication that can be called 'specific' in the arrest of the
mechanism of narcotic drug addiction-disease. There is
no more of a specific remedy for narcotic drug addiction
than there is for typhoid or pneumonia. The wide ad-
vertisement of treatments based on supposed 'specific'
action of the products of the belladonna and hyoscyamus
and similar groups is unfortunate. They have in my
opinion, no action as curative agents in narcotic drug
addiction-disease which can entitle them to consideration
as specific or special curative remedies. The drugs of this
group are useful in many cases, intelligently applied to
meet therapeutic indications. They exhibit wide varia-
tion of action and reaction in narcotic drug addicts at
different clinical stages and under different clinical conditions, and their dosage presents an extremely wide range
of individual measure. They are dangerous drugs in the
hands of the inexpert or careless, or used in a routine
manner or dosage. The status which they have acquired
as specific medication in narcotic addiction disease I hold
to be a medical fallacy which should be strongly opposed
and early remedied."

The search for panaceas, specifics and routine treatments has constituted a stage in the therapeutic history
of most disease conditions. It marks the effort to make
wide and general application of a partial comprehension

of facts and imperfect recognition of fundamentals and is successful only as an individual case is occasionally capable of responding, perhaps by clinical accident, to the specific routine employed.

Undue insistence and publicity secured for or given to a procedure of this description, is a real obstacle to the development of clinical and scientific understanding of the condition treated. It distracts attention from broad clinical consideration of disease itself, from scientific investigation into pathology and disease mechanism, from determination and observation of fundamental facts, whose comprehension and analysis form the essential factor in the widespread successful handling of any condition, and from proper conception and appreciation of the addiction patient and the addiction problem as a whole with its many and varied aspects.

Various procedures in themselves, however, are not to be utterly discredited and condemned. They have performed a function in a transitional stage of education and progress. They can all bring evidence in support of some "cures." In their origin and inception they represent honest effort, study and original thought. In analysis of them can be seen, in the minds of those who first evolved them, recognition and application of one or another of the basic elements, reactions or facts of addiction-disease. Each generation builds upon and adds to the work of the previous one, discards or adopts according to its more complete knowledge. We are building upon the various procedures of the past just as our successors will build upon our work of the present and will discard or adopt our various instruments and theories.

We are nearing the end of consideration of routinely applied procedures, in all diseases. In addiction we are entering upon a stage of attitude and handling in which there shall be in each case comprehension of intrinsic elements and appreciation of their relative importance, and in which there shall be competent interpretation of symptomatology and competent selection and application of therapeutic measures, placing our efforts on a rational basis and adapting handling and treatment to the needs of the individual.

Our stumbling-block in the past has been that our minds have been too much focused upon the mere use of narcotic drug and upon the stopping of drug use and too little upon the individual we were treating and the mechanism of his disease. We have tended to apply our remedial efforts to narcotic use instead of to narcotic drug addiction-disease.

This may explain the paucity of clinical and scientific information as to addiction-disease coming from the institutions in which these cases are gathered. It seems to be the fact that the narcotic wards of our great charity hospitals and institutions of custody and correction still in great measure proceed with their handling of narcotic addicts on the basis of mental or moral degeneracy or deficiency or weakness of will, or morbid appetite, etc., or apply one or another of the various remedies or combinations of remedies. Their internes and nurses do not seem to graduate with a conception of addiction as a definite physical disease, with clinically significant symptomatology and constant physical reactions and phenomena. That these institutions have after many years given us so little information as to the definite physical symptoms and phenomena which their patients constantly manifest is in large measure the result of attention directed to control of drug use instead of to alleviation of physical addiction-disease. There has been much discussion over various methods of treatment and over measures for the control of patient and of narcotic drug, and there has been insufficient study and analysis of the clinical details of addiction-disease manifestations and their possible therapeutic significance.

There has been of late, however, signs of change in

this situation, and in this change lies one of the greatest
hopes of solution of the narcotic drug problem.   The attitude towards addiction is beginning to follow the trend
of modern medicine in getting away from special or
routine treatments, and the search for specifics and panaceas, and in aiming at and devoting great effort to the
searching out, consideration of, and treatment of fundamental cause and underlying condition.   When this
method of approach is applied widely to addiction-disease, and the facilities of our great hospitals and institutions of research properly directed to its furtherance,
there will come a re-arrangement of conception of opiate
addiction.   Restraint and custodial care, and psychologic
and psychiatric classification will be applied more spar-
ingly.   Many worthy sick people will — instead of being
refused treatment, or turned back upon their own resources after inadequate treatment — thus adding to the
public and private burden of the care of the unfit — be
rationally treated as sick people and returned to health
and self-supporting competency.

The one great point to be kept in mind is that narcotic
addicts are sick; sick of a definite and now demonstrable
disease.   This disease is variously complicated and widely
variable as it occurs in individual patients.   Although
some individuals, afflicted with this disease, may require
custodial or correctional handling — the fundamental
physical disease cannot be properly arrested nor handled
successfully by mental, moral, sociological or penological
methods only.   Any toxic, worried, fear-ridden or suffering sick man may show psychological or even psychiatrical manifestations or complications, but observing and
attempting to control complications only will not cure
basic disease.

Even if it should some day develop that a serum can
be produced against the underlying toxins of addiction-
disease; and this is not beyond the bounds of possibility;

its usefulness and application must remain for the present matters of academic speculation.   Other than this possibility, there seems practically no hope of a properly called " specific medication " in narcotic drug addiction-disease.   Even with its discovery, it is highly improbable that a routine treatment applicable to all cases could ever be successfully adopted.   In the very few disease conditions in which we can properly be said to have " specific " medication, routine handling and treatment of all cases is inadvisable and unsatisfactory.

There is not and probably never will be any specific routine treatment successfully applicable to all cases of any complex and variable disease condition.   We shall save much public money, and personal effort and time, and shall save the narcotic addict much suffering and discouragement, and shall add much to human health, competency and happiness when we realize these facts as applied to addiction-disease, and proceed upon them in a spirit of broad humanity and of rational clinical study and remedy of obvious disease symptomatology.   Narcotic drug addiction-disease is a definite, and in most cases arrestable disease.   It should be widely so regarded and studied and treated.

CHAPTER VI

If anything has been demonstrated conclusively concerning narcotics it is that the methods of the past, legal, administrative, and medical, have not solved the narcotic drug problem, nor controlled the narcotic drug situation, nor been successful in the handling of the narcotic drug addict.

Some factor or element of great and fundamental importance has obviously been neglected. This lacking element is general recognition of the presence of disease processes which cause the symptomatology and phenomena of body-need for opiate drug. One of the essentials for the practical solution and management of the narcotic drug problem is the realization by the medical profession, legislators, administrators and laity that opiate drug addiction is a definite disease entity, to be treated as such, and calling for extensive clinical and laboratory investigation and study such as have been accorded other diseases over which we have gained the mastery. One of the most needed achievements in the line of practical remedy is the admission of narcotic drug addiction-disease to its legitimate place as an accepted part of the practice of internal medicine and the stimulating of education concerning it among medical practitioners, medical students and nurses.

As was stated in the last chapter, too much emphasis has been placed on drug use and drug withdrawal, as if the drug itself were the most important element in the clinical picture of addiction. In the handling and treatment of addiction-disease it should be constantly borne in mind that the ultimate withdrawal of opiate from the addict is simply one stage, and not by any means the most important consideration in his rational handling. Its management in most cases is a matter of scientific clinical certainty and satisfactory accomplishment by the physician who understands the disease he is treating and who is clinically proficient in the control of its elements by indicated therapeutic procedure. The ease of handling the stage of final withdrawal, the extent to which suffering, nervous strain and exhaustion can be avoided in it, and its final issue depend greatly upon the physical and reactive condition of the man from whom drug is withdrawn. Like the stage of crisis in pneumonia, its course and conduct and results are largely influenced by the condition in which the patient approaches the withdrawal. It is of vastly more importance to measure and control reactions and treat a patient so as to get him into the fittest possible condition for final withdrawal and rapid convalescence, than it is to focus attention on the mere reduction or withdrawal of drug, or on the mere amount of drug used. Final withdrawal of drug, like an operation of election, is to be done when the patient is in the fittest condition and ready for it. With the addict who is well nourished, non-inhibited, and physically and glandularly reactive, it can be accomplished with little or no discomfort, in a very short time, leaving practically nothing to demand a protracted and difficult stage of convalescence or of so-called " after care."

It becomes evident, therefore, that the handling of an opiate addict, preliminary to withdrawal of the drug to which he is addicted is of greatest importance. The ease of withdrawal and rapidity and completeness of subsequent recuperation, is largely commensurate with the extent of organic dependence upon the drug and the physical condition of the patient. One man using the same amount as another is dependent upon its effects for the support of his organic processes to a much greater extent. The evident solution lies in a preliminary stage, removing inhibition, reducing in so far as possible organic and functional dependence upon drug, and putting the patient into the best possible reactive condition. I believe that in many cases it is imperative for successful issue to train the patient for the shock and strain of opiate withdrawal and in practically all other cases, though less imperative, most desirable.

It has been objected that this will prolong treatment. My experience has been that it very much facilitates withdrawal treatment, and not only renders it easier and more uniformly successful and complete, but that it tends to shorten and make less troublesome, and in some cases practically eliminates, convalescence.

I have therefore instituted as an important part of my procedure, a Preliminary Stage of study and handling and treatment of my patient before attempting withdrawal of the drug. During this time I study my patient, regarding him not simply as a narcotic addict but as a sick man to be investigated as carefully as a cardiac or any other patient, and all his organic and functional conditions appreciated, and all of his functional and glandular actions estimated in their competency and balance and their reactions both to the drug of addiction and to the influences of addiction disease mechanism. Conditions long masked by opiates, and forgotten, even by the patient himself, may seriously affect treatment, convalescence and prognosis if undetected before withdrawal is instituted. Their relations to and possible influence upon addiction and its treatment, and fully as important — the possible effect of treatment and withdrawal of drug upon them, should be very carefully estimated. If advisable or possible they should be remedied before withdrawal of the drug of addiction.

Also such mental or psychical disturbances as may exist in a given case should be traced to their origin, estimated and reckoned with. Very often they will be found to be not inherent but a result of past suffering and present worry and fear. The patient's confidence in his physician's ability to treat the disease from which he suffers should be strengthened, and his doubts and fears allayed. Addiction patients are well informed concerning opiates and are acquainted with the manifestations of addiction-disease, and have had experience with or full information concerning the various methods of cure. They are, like any other chronic sick person, suspiciously and keenly analytic of themselves and of the physician, and unless handled with appreciation of their condition are naturally the prey of constant worry and fear. Co-operation and confidence between patient and physician vastly influence the amount of nervous energy expended by both, and in this, as in other diseases are big factors in treatment and in convalescence.

Another advantage of a preliminary stage is one which has been too little considered, but which will before long come to demand the same intelligent attention and measure as is given to the contemplation of operations in and treatment for chronic other conditions. It is this — in what condition will withdrawal of opiate even though skillfully conducted and successfully accomplished, leave the individual in his value to himself, and to his family and to the community, in view of co-existing physical conditions? Withdrawal of opiate drug has been in not a few cases the cause of transforming of a capable and useful citizen into an invalid incompetent, for whose ultimate salvation and competent physical and mental function and organic and glandular control resumption of opiate medication was determined to be a therapeutic necessity.

Such considerations as this should be all taken, analyzed

and estimated in a preliminary stage and if treatment is only going to injure a patient he should be instructed how to handle his addiction, and advised to continue his opiate medication, and not be subjected to useless expense and trials.

Basic Principles of Addiction-disease Handling

Intelligent addicts well know that, other factors being equal, the less number of times in a day they take their drug, the less inhibited, the less constipated and more normal they are, and the smaller amount of narcotic drug they require to maintain them physically and mentally competent.   It is unfortunate that this therapeutic principle so widely recognized among intelligent addicts has not received full recognition and therapeutic employment by all of those who handle and treat addiction-disease.   Its probable explanation is very simple — apparently a period of inhibition follows the administration of narcotic or opiate drugs; and the length of this period is not in ratio to the size of the dose administered.   Consequently, the fewer number of times in a day a dose of narcotic drug is administered, the greater amount of competent metabolism is present — the more adequate is the patient's elimination and nutrition — the smaller amount of opiate or its product lies stored in inhibited and atonic cells, and the smaller amount of antidotal substance is manufactured for the protection of the body, and to some extent, the smaller amount of opiate is required.

In caring for the narcotic addict, therefore, one of the most important therapeutic measures is the regulation of the interval of his narcotic drug administration.   I have repeatedly experimented upon addicts who were not confined or under restraint in any way.   I explained to them the inhibitory effects of too frequent dosage and instructed them to use the amount of drug they found necessary for twenty-four hours in larger doses at longer intervals.

This procedure alone, in many cases transforms the pallid, starved, constipated and deteriorated addict within a surprisingly short time into a well-nourished, well-reactive and practically normally functionating individual. With the return of health, vitality, and normal nutrition and elimination, his body requires still less drug and he voluntarily and without mental struggle and nervous strain reduces the amount of drug used. I wish to emphasize that in these experimental cases there were no other therapeutic measures employed in the way of medication.

The practical therapeutic application of wide-interval administration of opiate drug is made possible by the fact that the narcotic addict can tolerate without harm large doses of the drug of addiction. It is made controllable by the fact, that, within certain limits, the length of time over which a dose of narcotic drug will maintain a patient in narcotic drug balance — or free from the symptomatology of drug need — is in mathematical ratio to the size of the dose administered. Each addict requires, under the conditions of his daily life at a given time, to satisfy the demands of his physical addiction-disease mechanism, and to maintain him in narcotic drug balance, an amount of drug which can be estimated in terms of twenty-four hours and which I have called the amount of minimum daily need. The most important consideration in the administration of narcotic drug to a narcotic addict is to supply the amount of minimum daily need and maintain narcotic drug balance with the least inhibition of function.

Failure to maintain narcotic drug balance and a degree below the amount of minimum daily need renders the addict functionally and physically incompetent. He is in a condition of physical and nerve incapacity and exhaustion. He has no physical tone; he has markedly impaired circulation; he cannot react, he has no recuperative powers; he has constantly in his body, according to modern theory, unneutralized autogenous poison which robs him of vitality, reaction and functional efficiency even though it may not be present in sufficient amounts to give rise to the violent spectacular and agonizing manifestations of complete narcotic deprivation. In other words, as I have written elsewhere, " the reduction of the drug of addiction below the amount of body-need robs the addict of his most valuable asset in securing and maintaining recuperative powers." In no other disease would an intelligent physician persist in the application of measures which robbed his patient of recuperative powers and expect satisfactory issue of the case he was trying to treat. Until the physician and patient are ready and prepared for the institution of the stage of final withdrawal of drug, the patient should never be allowed to drop below the amount of minimum daily need in his opiate intake.

It is evident therefore, that upon the intelligent and competent estimation, measure and control of physical narcotic drug balance and inhibition of function depend the reaction, well being and therapeutic progress of the man who has narcotic drug addiction-disease. These factors also markedly influence the action of all medication, including the drug of addiction, upon the body of the opiate addict. They influence the reaction of the addict's body to all medication. Medication cannot be intelligently administered to the opiate addict unless those who administer it have understanding and clinical appreciation of the widely varying reaction of the addict under different conditions of drug balance and inhibition of function. Failure to recognize and appreciate this fact explains a considerable portion of the past failures and the past mortality attending specific and special methods and treatments, and so-called " cures." The dosage of medication administered and the time of its administration should therefore be determined upon with watchful eye to the reaction of the patient, and with intelligent comprehension of the possibilities in reactionary change.

The actions and the dosage of therapeutic agents have been largely determined by experimentation on individuals and animals of average normal reaction. The toxic, the inhibited and the narcotic addicted do not display the normal reaction to therapeutic agents. Under some conditions they over-react both physically and nervously, and under other conditions they under-react. Detailed consideration of this matter is not possible in this book. It offers for investigation a field well worthy of exploration both clinical and laboratory. It will only state that as the manifestations and influences of toxemia, functional exhaustion, inhibition, and, in the addicted, of varying physical drug balance, have become increasingly definite and tangible and capable of clinical measure and determination, my medication of the toxic and the exhausted and the inhibited individual, as well as of the narcotic addicted, has become progressively more effective. These observations apply to conditions other than opiate drug addiction, and are worthy of consideration in all toxic, and exhaustion and depression states.

I have already spoken of the imperative physical need for the drug of addiction. I have also referred to the amount of minimum daily need for the drug of addiction. The recognition of factors which influence these is of great importance. Many of these factors are so commonplace and so obvious in their relation to the extent of body need that they are appreciated by most intelligent addicts. Anything which increases the expenditure of physical and nervous energy increases the addict's need for opiate drug. Among the most potent influences are worry, fear and physical suffering. They consume physical fuel; and an important part of the addict's physical fuel is the drug of his addiction. In addition to this, worry and fear and suffering are also markedly inhibitory of glandular and peristaltic function.   The expenditure of energy in mental and muscular work also calls for increased supply of the drug of addiction.   I need not enlarge upon this important fact.   Its application to the handling and treatment of the addict is evident.   Narcotic drug should be supplied to meet the physical needs of the individual case, and only be decreased as intelligent handling of the factors which determine that need have lessened it.

The method of gradual reduction of dose to the point of ultimate discontinuance is practical and feasible under conditions and at an expense of time and money which are possible to but very few addicts.   The forcible reduction of dose without regard to the environmental, mental, economic, physical or other conditions of the average and individual addict, and absolutely ignoring the considerations of the mechanism and symptomatology of his addiction-disease is barbarous, harmful and futile.   Enforced reduction of dose below the point of body need is not worth what it costs in nerve-strain, suffering, and physical inadequacy.   The extent of addiction-disease and the degree of progress in its remedy cannot be measured in terms of amount of drug administered.   It must be measured in terms of clinical symptomatology, just as progress is measured in any other disease.   Reduction of dose below the amount of body need, prior to the stage of final withdrawal, constitutes a serious therapeutic handicap and is most decidedly contra-indicated.   Withdrawal of opiate from an addict whose physical reaction and strength and nerve force have been reduced and depleted by continued reduction of amount of drug without commensurate reduction in the extent of body need is harder than withdrawal from a reactive individual with reserve nerve and physical force who may be taking a much larger dose.

The average addict must support himself and his family. His physical well-being and economic efficiency should be considerations in the welfare of the community in which he lives. Legislative and other investigation has shown that we are entirely unequipped both institutionally and professionally for the successful immediate withdrawal of opiate from even a small proportion of our present census of the opiate addicted. In view therefore, of the practical impossibility of immediate successful withdrawal treatment, and in view of what is known and can be demonstrated and taught in the accomplishment of final withdrawal, I do not hesitate to state that, until we are prepared and in a position to skillfully and competently handle the stage of final withdrawal to assured successful issue, it is much wiser to supply to the addict who is not a public menace the drug of his addiction to the extent of his physical needs, and to teach him how to use the drug of addiction in such a way as will maintain his physical and economic efficiency, than it is by enforced reduction of dose to deprive him for a long time of working ability and his family of his support. Furthermore, the addict who is insufficiently supplied with the opiate of his addiction, turns in desperation to the use of things far more harmful to him than the drug of his addiction. This he does in the vain hope of obtaining mental and nervous and physical stimulus and support and some surcease of his misery. The many wrecks of addicts to be seen trying through insufficient supply of narcotic drug, self-poisoned with other drugs which they have purchased, alcohol, bromides, coal tar products, cocaine, and of late hyoscine — their addiction disease unrelieved and undiminished — are sufficient argument against mere reduction of dose, below physical body need.

The personal attitude of the physician towards opiate addicted patients is of great importance. The medical man who is to treat a case suffering from addiction-disease successfully to the end of relieving this condition, or who is treating addiction-disease as an intercurrent condition complicating another disease, must first of all make

his patient realize that the physician himself knows something about addiction as a disease.   He must never give
his patient any hint or reason to suspect that he regards
opiate addiction as a habit, a vice, a degrading indulgence
which can be to any curative or even therapeutic extent,
combatted by the exercise of will-power.

In their desperation and ignorance, the vast majority
of addicts have repeatedly exercised will-power in self-
denial of their drug to the limits of their physical endurance, and they know the futility and suffering of attempts based simply and solely upon the exercise of will-
power.   Experience has taught them actual facts concerning the physical action of narcotic drugs and concerning
the results of insufficient supply of narcotic drug in a man
who is addicted.   The addict knows that he does not take
a drug because he enjoys it.   He knows that he experiences no sensuous gratification or other pleasure from its
administration.   He knows that he uses a narcotic drug
simply and solely because he has to use it to escape physical
incompetence and physical agony.   As I said before, almost without exception the narcotic addict has proceeded
of his own accord, or under the direction and advice of
others, on the theory of exercising will power, and resist-
ing temptation.   With the few exceptions of those made
in a very early stage and before addiction mechanism had
become strongly developed and rooted in his physical
processes, such efforts on the basis of this theory have
been useless.

It is practically impossible to argue successfully on the
basis of theory with the man who has experienced facts.
Narcotic addiction furnishes a class of patients who know
more about their own disease than any other class of
people.   They can accurately estimate the extent of understanding and knowledge possessed by the man who is
treating them, and they are desperately critical.   Almost
without exception, except for some of the true " under-

world," they desire above all else to escape from their condition. I know that this is not the popular conception and for the present may be by some regarded as heresy. Therefore, it is of essential importance that between the doctor who treats an addict of average intelligence and that addict must exist co-operation and understanding. As soon as this patient realizes two things — that the doctor does not believe his expressed wish to be cured, and that he interprets the patient's desire for relief from suffering as simply a desire for more opiate and the expression of habit, vice or degraded appetite which should be controlled by the exercise of " will-power," — there is an end to that patient's confidence in that doctor, and to the help that that doctor can give to that patient. As I have written elsewhere, the opiate addict of average intelligence will co-operate with his medical adviser to the extent of his physical endurance, so long as he has any belief in that adviser's understanding of his condition, and ability to help him.

In my own work, and as a result of my own experience I have found that as a rule the extent to which an intelligent addiction patient cooperates with me has been a measure of the understanding and technical ability with which I handled him, rather than a measure of his desire to be helped. It is held by many that a majority of addiction-patients are not possessed of average intelligence and are not honest in their statements. I will simply say that even in the Alcoholic and Prison Wards of Bellevue and in the narcotic wards of the New York Workhouse Hospital I came more and more to seek in faults of medical and nursing handling the explanation of apparent lack of cooperation. In the Annual Report of the New York Department of Correction for 1915, in commenting upon the work of the narcotic wards, is stated, " In ratio as there has been at any given time among our interne and nursing staff comprehension and understanding of the manifestations and underlying principles of narcotic drug addiction-disease and of its rational handling in the individual case, our results have been good or bad."

Several years ago I wrote as follows: " As to the existing opinion that the morphinist does not want to be cured and that while under treatment he cannot be trusted and will not cooperate·but will secretly secure and use his drug, I can only quote from personal experience with these cases. During my early attempts, my patients, beginning with the best intentions in the world, often tried to beg, steal or get in any possible way, the drug of their addiction. Like others I placed the blame upon their supposed weakness of will and lack of determination to get rid of their malady. Later I realized the fact that the blame rested entirely upon the shoulders of my medical inefficiency and my lack of understanding and ability to observe and interpret my patient's condition. The morphinist as a rule will cooperate and will suffer to the limit of his endurance. Demanding cooperation of a case of morphinism during and following incompetent withdrawal of the drug is much like asking a man to cooperate for an indefinite period in his own torture. There is a limit to every one's power of endurance of suffering."

Of primary importance, then, if a physician, institutional or practitioner, is to have any success in handling a case of opiate addiction-disease, is his attitude towards his patient — divesting himself of all conception of habit, appetite or vice as explanation of characteristic physical manifestations and symptomatology, and approaching the patient as a man with a definite disease requiring and deserving intelligent clinical handling. The patient will be the very first to mark a physician's shortcomings. If he has not confidence in the doctor's ability and understanding of his illness the doctor can help him but little. This statement applies not to addiction-disease alone but to every medical condition.

There are three clinical demonstrable elements to be determined, measured and controlled in the actual therapeutic handling of cases of narcotic addiction-disease. The first of these is the actual amount of drug which the patient's body demands to maintain functional and organic efficiency and to escape physical distress. The second of these is the extent of auto- and intestinal-intoxication, autotoxicosis and malnutrition. The third of these, which is both a result of and a causative element in the other two, is the extent of inhibition of function.

In the successful handling of a case of addiction-disease, therefore, the first effort should be to determine approximately the amount of the patient's minimum daily physical need for the drug of his addiction. This need is clinically recognizable and definitely measurable. It should be met to whatever extent it is present so long as it exists, and dosage diminished only as competent treatment diminishes the extent of need. This physical need can be demonstrated and accurately measured by clean-cut symptomatology. It can be expressed in mathematical terms of amounts of drug required in twenty-four hours. Work, worry, strain — anything which consumes physical or nervous energy increases this need. If this physical need is not met the patient is robbed of physical tone and physical reaction. He is robbed of metabolic balance and functional competency. He is, in short, robbed of the basic ability which his body has to regain health.

In the estimation of this amount of physical need the procedure is very simple. Have administered to the patient who is manifesting the symptomatology of drug-need, sufficient drug to remove the symptoms and restore him to complete physical, functional and nerve balance. Have the length of time observed which elapses before the symptoms of drug need reappear. Have this repeated several times and information is secured as to what quantity of opiate under the existing conditions will hold that patient in drug-balance for a known length of time. In this way can be mathematically estimated the extent of physical drug-need. The average need for twenty-four hours can be easily computed from the data obtained. It is merely a matter of arithmetic.

The regulation of dosage can also be estimated with approximate accuracy. As has been stated before, the interval of freedom from withdrawal manifestations is found to be, in a general way and within certain limits, in ratio to the size of the dosage. For example, if in a given case, under given conditions of fear, worry, physical or nervous strain, pain, etc., as discussed elsewhere — one grain of morphine will last a given patient at a given time for four hours; under the same conditions two grains will last for approximately eight hours. There are limits to the application of this rule. It is stated as the general operating of an addiction-disease phenomenon which is useful as a therapeutic guide.

The amount of actual physical body need as capable of approximate estimation in the above manner should be administered to the patient, any reduction being guided by the fact that his clinical symptomatology and physical manifestations demonstrate that the amount required by his addiction-disease has been reduced. It is much wiser for the progress of the average addiction case to have the drug administered in the amount of estimated physical need than it is to attempt to reduce the amount of drug before his reactions show reduction in physical drug-need. The success of outcome and the measure of progress in such a case is not to be estimated by the amount of drug the patient is receiving, but is to be measured by the patient's condition and clinical manifestations. The mere fact that a physician has reduced a narcotic addict's opiate intake from a large dosage to a very small dosage, or indeed has denied him any opiate at all for a considerable length of time, is no evidence that he is curing or has cured his patient of addiction-disease. Unless the physical mechanism of body-need for an opiate has been completely and actually quieted, the patient may have in his body for perhaps weeks and months after the last administration of the drug, a physical demand for it. *The taking of opiate does not constitute opiate addiction-disease.* Also the mere fact that an addict is no longer taking opiate does not constitute proof that he is "cured" of opiate addiction. The non-recognition of this fact lies at the root of much past failure. The general axiomatic statement might be that an addict should be supplied with the drug of his addiction to the complete extent of his physical need at any given time until conditions are right for the undertaking of assuredly competent opiate withdrawal and complete arrest of his addiction-disease mechanism.

The mere amount of drug used by a patient in twenty-four hours is a matter of minor importance compared with the general health, physical tone, nervous glandular and functional balance, reaction and resistance of that patient. Also the amount of drug taken by a patient in twenty-four hours is absolutely no adequate measure of the strength or stage of development of his addiction-disease. If he does not get enough opiate he cannot competently functionate; he cannot be adequately nourished; he cannot sufficiently eliminate. He is subjected to the influences of constant discomfort and nerve strain in the endurance of low-grade withdrawal manifestations. He is worried and becoming exhausted. It becomes apparent that by continued maintainance of narcotic administration below the amount of physical body-drug-need the very factors are created which have been described as increasing body-drug-need. It is difficult to see any therapeutic advantage in such a situation. Moreover, as has been stated before, it is far easier to eradicate completely and successfully narcotic drug need in a short time and without marked discomfort, from a functionally competent and organically healthy man who is taking a physically sufficient amount, than it is from a nerve-racked, worried and physically, nervously, and functionally exhausted wreck who is under-dosed.

It is therefore much wiser to direct immediate efforts to the securing and maintaining of health, reaction and tone — irrespective of the amount of drug required — until there is time and opportunity for the undertaking of competent withdrawal — a stage of handling and treatment concerning whose physical and clinical phenomena and manifestations and dangers too few are educated to and familiar with.

In regulating the administration of drug as to size and intervals of dosage — amounts should be sufficient to allow the patient long intervals between doses. In the determination of this, it is necessary to study and experiment with the reactions in the individual case. The effort, however, should be to have the drug administered the smallest possible number of times in the twenty-four hours compatible with the patient's well-being. For example — if a given patient's daily need is three grains a day, it is much wiser to administer this amount of drug in doses of one grain three times a day or a grain and a half twice a day as soon as practicable, than it is to have it administered in larger numbers of smaller doses at more frequent intervals. The reason is, that, apparently after a dose of narcotic drug is administered function is inhibited for a length of time which is not in proportion to the size of the dose administered. On the other hand, as has been stated, within limits, the length of time over which a dose of narcotic drug will hold a patient in drug balance and free from the physical manifestations of drug need is in proportion to the size of the dose. Therefore large doses at wide intervals permit greatest freedom from functional inhibition and as well, if not better, supply the demands of physical drug need.

I have briefly referred to the elements of intestinal and autointoxication and autotoxicosis. Intestinal and autointoxication, combined with worry, fear, and anxiety, constitute very important causative and controlling factors in whatever mental and physical deterioration has taken place in a case of narcotic-drug-addiction-disease. Physical, mental and moral deterioration are to a very small extent direct results of narcotic drug action *per se*. As long as a narcotic drug addict is maintained non-toxic, uninhibited and unworried, he is practically at his individual normal, plus an added physical need. It should not be necessary to recall to memory many cases of upright, honorable and competent and apparently healthy men and women who have been narcotic addicts over very many years, unknown to but very few or none of their relatives or friends or even physicians. As has been stated before, their apparent immunity to the supposed stigmata of narcotic drug action was not due to the fact that they were on a higher mental or moral plane than their less fortunate fellows, or that they were possessed of sufficient will-power to resist temptation in the over-indulgence of their so-called appetite. The facts are that by experience they found out that if they used narcotic drug in amounts indicated by the manifestations of their disease, and did not take it too often and kept their bowels open and did not worry, they were as normal as anybody else except for the fact that they had to take a dose of a certain medicine two or three times a day. In other words they simply learned to manage their disease in a way to avoid complications. They met their issue squarely; they discounted theory and recognized facts, and they used common sense in the interpretation and application of what they learned.

The control of auto and intestinal intoxication in narcotic addiction is as a rule of easy accomplishment if the patient is uninhibited and in functional balance and is not over-supplied or under-supplied with the drug of his addiction. The narcotic addict who is non-toxic and in drug balance and is not harassed by worry or fear needs practically no more drastic methods of elimination than his non-addicted brother. If he is over-dosed his elimination is inhibited; if he is under-dosed his eliminative powers are not capable of response. The element in the securing of evacuation of the bowel in a drug case, as well as in a toxic case of whatever description, is sluggish peristalsis; in other words, it is inhibition of nervous impulse. It is therefore not necessary to load a bowel up with large amounts of drastic and irritating cathartics. Indeed this procedure is very harmful and abortive of ultimate results. An over-irritated intestinal tract is not a good eliminative organ. To my mind the so-called " typical stool," of the so-called " Towns Treatment " with its content of jelly mucus has no clinical significance other than its evidence of a production of an exhaustive and irritative mucous colitis and means that however much purging may be accomplished competent elimination from the colon is at an end. Its appearance in a case under my care I should regard as evidence of injudicious treatment. For the bowel elimination of a case of narcotic-addiction there is needed practically nothing beyond the ordinary mild and non-irritating catharsis. All that is needed is to remember that if inhibition of peristalsis has not as yet been overcome, you may be wise to administer, about the time you should get an evacuation, strychnine or other peristaltic stimulators in sufficient amounts to overcome existing inhibition and stimulate peristalsis.

Inhibition of function, as I have already shown, is a basic factor in the development and maintaining of the narcotic addiction-disease state. It is of great importance to recognize, estimate and control its presence and influence. Inhibition of function is due to nervous exhaustion from overwork, fear, anxiety and suffering; it follows for a few hours the administration of opiate drugs; it is a constant result of chronic constipation and of intestinal and auto-toxemia. The rationale of its control is evident from the enumeration of its causes. Until its causative factors have been removed or controlled, its manifestations must be treated symptomatically — remembering always that for therapeutic action in an inhibited individual dosage of medicinal agents varies, and must be estimated from clinical observation and experiment and not from memory of the text-books. To the man experienced in their use some of the internal secretory glandular products are at times helpful. As has been stated above, strychnine or other peristaltic stimulator is useful.

Finally I repeat again my disbelief in and opposition to the use of any drug or combination of drugs under the impression that they have or may have specific curative action against addiction-disease. Although I at times employ various of the drugs commonly mentioned in connection with the treatment of addiction, I do so with no belief that they have " specific " properties in this disease. I use them in the treatment of addiction as I do in other disease conditions, simply and solely as they meet individual clinical and therapeutic indications. Petty took this stand years ago. I do not regard these drugs as curative of addiction-disease, and I do not constantly use any of them.

I do not use or endorse, a " belladonna " treatment, a " hyoscine " treatment, nor any other description of specific or routine treatment in addiction-disease. I regard the drugs of the belladonna and hyoscyamus groups, pilocarpine, etc., as extremely dangerous drugs to be routinely or carelessly used in the treatment of addiction-disease. They are rendered safe only after personal experience and study into their action and appreciation of the factors and influences which control their action in the functional, toxic, and narcotic drug conditions. The routine and unintelligent use of the products of these groups of drugs in the treatment of narcotic addiction — under the mistaken impression that they somehow or other have direct curative action upon the disease condition — has been the cause of a considerable mortality and an easily understood opposition among intelligent addicts. Hyoscine or scopolamine and the other members of this group, ezerine, pilocarpine, the coal tar products, etc., are at times useful drugs to meet indications in the treatment of a case of addiction. Increasing intelligence in the handling of the addiction mechanism itself, however, renders the necessity of their use less and less frequent and the dosage of them required for therapeutic action smaller and smaller. They should simply be classed as of use among other things, peristaltic and circulatory stimulation and support, indicated eliminants, kindness and consideration, understanding and intelligence or any of the other therapeutic weapons in our possession.

Elimination and the securing of it in the narcotic addicted has been referred to in this chapter. The chapter should not be closed however, without a word of warning against the excessive purgation with drastic and over irritating agents employed by some in this condition. Drastic purgation is not at all synonymous with competent elimination. Competent elimination is not to be measured in terms of bowel-movements; but in terms of clinical symptomatology of toxemia, circulation and measure of functional efficiency. Excessive purgation means over-irritation and over-stimulation of eliminative mechanism, results in the interference with and exhaustion of function and defeats true elimination.

Presence of good circulatory tone and absence of congestion in the eliminative organs is to me one of the most important factors in true elimination. The addict who is in good functional tone, has competent circulation, is in narcotic drug balance, and is noninhibited, needs no more drastic eliminative measures than belong to ordinary rational therapeutics in the nonaddicted.

As to final withdrawal of the drug, and ultimate arrest of the disease, I shall say but little in this book.

I follow no " routine " and have no set procedure. I am guided, as in my handling of the other stages of addiction-disease, by the condition of my patient and his clinical requirements. There is no one procedure applicable to all cases of any condition in medicine and surgery. In narcotic addiction-disease, as in all other conditions of medicine and surgery, the man who will have the best results is the man who is possessed of the widest and most varied experience combined with intelligent observation, technical skill and clinical judgment in the selection of procedure best adapted to the needs of the individual case. Familiarity and experience with different methods and procedures reveals in each and nearly all of them some advantages and some defects. The wise man and the man whose results will most approach uniform success is he who can make intelligent selection and use of whatever is most applicable to the needs of the case he treats, either out of his own experience and discoveries, or out of his familiarity with the work of others.

An element in successful withdrawal of narcotic must also remain, as in everything else, the inherent personal gifts and qualifications of the individual operator. A man works best with the tools most adapted to his hand, and operators of different temperaments and of different experience and training will always disagree on points of procedure and technique. My own procedure in final withdrawal is determined largely by my study and measure of my patient and my patient's reactions, addiction and otherwise, during my preliminary or preparatory work, selecting the time for final withdrawal of drug by consideration of similar factors as would be taken into account in an operation of election.

After a preliminary stage, or stage of preparation, in which I have gotten rid of all possible abnormalities, physical and psychical, with my patient robust and reactive, confident and expectantly happy, with autointoxication, and inhibition removed and the possible residues of opiate or opiate product no longer stored in atonic body cells — the addiction-mechanism, therefore, only kept in activity by the current intake of opiate, which if properly handled and the patient not subjected to exhausting strain and struggle and suffering, can be eliminated in a very short time.   With these conditions consummated, I hasten elimination, keeping well away from exhausting purgation, maintaining my patient's circulatory and other functions, and conducting as rapid a withdrawal as is compatible with my patient's reactive condition and the reactions of his disease.

In other words, I endeavor by my conduct of the case to reverse the process of development of the physical addiction-disease with its concomitants and complications, as I find it in the individual case, arresting the addiction-disease mechanism only after I have cleared the clinical picture in so far as possible of all other considerations.

In a majority of cases by experienced choice of clinical procedure, combined with judgment and technical skill, the arrest of addiction-mechanism and the restoration of the narcotic addict to health and freedom from both opiate need and thought of opiate drug is a matter of assured accomplishment attended by little if any nervous strain and physical suffering.

Ability to accomplish this is not beyond the power of any competent practitioner, whether he reside in a hospital or is in private practice.   All that is required is instruction or information as to the mechanism of addiction-disease, clinical demonstration of its manifestations and reactions and the same amount of experience in their handling as is expected of a man who treats any other disease.

I have purposely refrained in this book from discussion of technical details of therapeutic procedures, and of various medications, and of their various indications, contra-indications, applications, dosage, etc. Such discussion, to be adequate and competent, would require much space and would distract from the general presentation of the problem, which is the purpose of this volume.

I have learned from experience in teaching and in treatment of cases that before there has been established appreciation of the whole personal and clinical problem and picture, and conception of its disease mechanism, and ability clinically to recognize and interpret symptomatology, discussion of technical details is premature and misleading.

CHAPTER VII

It is a common idea in the minds of both surgeons and physicians that an addict to narcotic drug is a difficult case for surgical handling and is a poor surgical risk. Numerous instances of surgeons refusing to operate upon a narcotic addict until the addict should have " stopped " the use of the drug, voice the almost prevailing attitude.

Very many, if not most, internists and practitioners view with gravest concern the presence of addiction in a serious illness coming under their care.

That the addict has borne this undeserved reputation as a poor surgical and medical risk, and that this reputation has been seemingly merited by previous medical and surgical experience, is not to be laid at the door of the existence of addiction in the patient. It is to be laid at the door of insufficient medical comprehension of addiction-disease and its mechanism in its material manifestations, and in its functional and organic influences, and at the door of inadequate clinical study into the analysis, estimation and control of these. Like much else that has been for generations generally accepted as true about narcotic drug addiction, the belief is erroneous that the addict is a poor surgical and medical risk because he is an addict.

As a surgeon once stated " These addicts have no resistance, and they go right out." Swayed by the old conception of addiction, this more than ordinarily humane and generous-hearted man had not the slightest suspicion as to why the addicts that he had operated upon had displayed

85

no resistance and had tended to " go right out." He had
in his mind simply the then prevailing and practically
unquestioned conception of the narcotic addict, and he had
not the slightest suspicion that a definite physical disease,
whose mechanism should have received intelligent clinical
handling and control was complicating the surgical cases
of the addicts who went right out. He had based, as all
of us once did, his opiate medication on his materia medica
conception of therapeutic dosage instead of on the demands
of an addiction-disease mechanism. It is rumored that
more than one illustrious life, full of past accomplishment
and potential future benefit to humanity and society, has
ended in this way.

The above statements do not apply to surgery alone.
They are equally true of medical conditions. Dominated
by their teachings as to opiate dosage in ordinary therapeutics, and by the older " habit " conception of addiction,
with little or no instruction as to the dosage indications
of addiction-disease, most practitioners, institutional and
private, do not adequately conceive and have no basis for
determination of opiate dosage in this disease. They do
not believe that the addict physically needs nor do many
of them realize that the addict can physically tolerate what
seems to them such dangerous and lethal amounts, and
they tend to ascribe his statements of usual dosage to
mental " cravings " to which they refuse to pander. Many
appreciate that such patients have often to be very carefully watched to prevent their suicide and that many of
them die, but fail to comprehend that these events may
be ascribed to inability to longer endure the suffering and
physical incompetency of body-need for opiate medication.

The recent epidemic of influenza and pneumonia furnishes examples of the importance of recognizing addiction-disease mechanism in intercurrent diseases. A number of instances have come to my attention. One of them
is of particular interest because of the graphic picture

presented by a series of sphygmographic tracings showing the physical organic dependence upon opiate in the circulation of an addict. It may be said in passing that these tracings and others made upon addicts in partial or complete opiate withdrawal parallel similar tracings by other clinical observers, and also those made by experimental laboratory workers upon addicted dogs.

The subject of these tracings was a man well-known and prominent in his community, 63 years of age, suffering from pneumonia with marked and persisting cardiac and circulatory deficiency which did not respond to the administration of the usual circulatory stimulants even in very large doses. I was called in consultation. Found the patient very weak and exhausted, with facial expression of protracted suffering and anxiety and despondency. Morphine in usual therapeutic doses had been daily administered for relief of pain, restlessness and sleeplessness, being insufficient however to control those manifestations. Pulse was, as shown in tracing number 1, very weak and intermittent. It was impossible to account for the whole clinical picture and history on the grounds of a typical pneumonia, present or resolving. Opiate addiction was suspected and the patient questioned. He had been suffering from opiate addiction-disease for many years, his addiction developing unsuspected by him as a result of medication for a painful and protracted condition many years previous. He begged to be allowed to die without his wife and son being told of his affliction. The following tracings made upon him are very instructive and significant, and cannot be interpreted upon any grounds of psychical explanation of addiction phenomena.

The last dose of morphine prior to these tracings was one-eighth of a grain given at 3:30 P. M.

First tracing (number 1) was made about 6:00 P. M.

Tracings 2, 3 and 4 were made at about fifteen minute

(Chart of Sphygmographic Tracings)

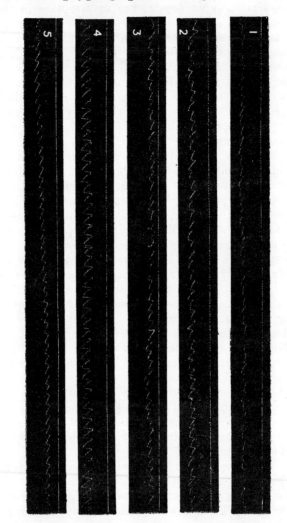

intervals. They were made following experimental hypodermic injections of morphine sulphate to determine the
extent of opiate need and organic dependence upon opiate
medication, and the amount of opiate required to restore
organic function and tone.

Tracing number 4, taking into consideration the
asthenic and exhaustion condition of the patient, shows
full support to circulation with some overaction.

Tracing number 5 was taken an hour or two after tracing number 4 to determine the holding power of the
dosage administered, after the circulation had reacted
from the immediate stimulation of the opiate medication.
This tracing, interpreted and considered together with
the clinical manifestations at the time, was decided to
be about normal for that patient at that time.

This patient would have died, not from pneumonia with
cardiac complications, but from insufficient control of the
mechanism of opiate addiction-disease.

On balanced and indicated daily morphine dosage,
patient made very rapid recovery and has continued well
and active.

Such cases as this, where addiction-disease co-exists or
is intercurrent with other medical or with surgical conditions, are not as uncommon as may be supposed. That
they are frequently unrecognized the histories of many
narcotic addicts demonstrates, and is discussed later.
Board of Health and Insurance mortality statistics are
undoubtedly very incomplete upon this situation. Addiction, regarded as a habit or indulgence, may easily be
overlooked or disregarded as a cause of death, direct or
contributing. It may easily be omitted from returns
made out, however actually important a part in the final
issue may have been played by the influences, upon body
function and upon physical resistance and recuperation,
of an unappreciated and inadequately controlled addiction-disease.

It is earlier stated that the common idea of the addict to narcotic drugs as a poor risk is an undeserved reputation, and is not to be laid at the door of addiction existence itself. In very many cases of opiate addiction, the opposite of the popular belief is true. The opiate addict, if his addiction mechanism is competently appreciated, its reactions accurately estimated, and its influences wisely controlled, is quite other than a bad risk. Indeed the mechanism of addiction and the opiate which caused it can often be handled in such a way in the control of glandular, circulatory, nervous and other function and reaction as to aid in the carrying over of emergencies, medical and surgical. A case in point is an emergency operation on the pancreas, performed upon a man in extremis, whose unexpected recovery and convalescence astonished all observers by being remarkably rapid and uncomplicated, due unquestionably in large part to the early recognition and clinical handling of his addiction-disease, and the possibilities it created for unusual opiate medication.

It has been my experience at times, when called in medical consultation upon post-operative cases whose lack of repair and slowness of recovery could not be accounted for, to discover an unsuspected addiction, and to find that the lack of repair and slowness of recovery was due simply and slowly to the want of comprehension of, or to inadequate control of addiction mechanism existing in the patient.

Many opiate addicts when about to undergo operation, have provided for possible contingencies by the concealment of, or by outside provision for, a supply of opiate sufficient in amount to meet their physical needs. There are very many addicts who have, out of their past experience and study upon themselves, competently controlled their own narcotic-drug-disease during treatment for other conditions, operative or medical. The number of narcotic addicts is not few who have been cared for medically with nursing attention, or have undergone operations for the remedy of various surgical conditions, have recovered, convalesced and been discharged without the physician or surgeon becoming aware that his patient was addicted. This is not a comment in criticism upon my professional brethren. In my own experience such a case is a matter of quite recent occurrence. A patient treated by me in a hospital, for conditions other than addiction, one day unexpectedly revealed to me the fact of long standing addiction. The patient had been afraid to tell me about this condition until thoroughly convinced of my attitude towards it, and had secured opiate medication elsewhere.

It seems strange that a condition of as powerful influence over body function and metabolism as is exerted by the addiction mechanism of narcotic drug-disease should not long ago have received exhaustive and complete clinical and laboratory study along the lines of its manifestations and influences, as well as along the line of reduction and deprivation of the drug of addiction. In view of the above it would seem to be of vastly more importance at the present time that the mass of practitioners of surgery as well as of medicine should understand and be able to control action and reaction in a narcotic addict as a result of his addiction-disease mechanism, than it is that they should attempt the mere reduction or denial of the drug of addiction.

Appreciation of the above would make available to narcotic addicts, suffering from other conditions, hospital and professional treatment and remedy of those conditions. Under present prevailing conceptions of addiction, many honest and worthy people addicted to opiates dare not avail themselves of needed treatment for medical conditions or operation for surgical conditions because of their uncertainty regarding the attitude towards and handling of addiction-disease existing in and carried out by the institution or practitioner to whom they would ordinarily appeal for help. The addict lives in constant fear of some injury or illness which may necessitate his coming into the hands of those whose conception of addiction is not in accord with the addict's experience of addiction-disease facts.

As I have emphasized in previous chapters, the actual withdrawing of opiate from an addict is simply one stage, and by no means the most important stage in the rational consideration and handling of a case of narcotic drug addiction. The fact that a patient is using an opiate drug, and that he uses, within reasonable limits, a larger or smaller amount of that drug, is a matter of very minor importance as compared with his general functional, nutritional, and metabolic efficiency. This is true as a general proposition in the handling of any case of narcotic drug addiction, and is vastly more true in the handling of cases of other conditions or diseases, operative or otherwise, that are complicated by narcotic drug addiction-disease. The physician or surgeon should realize that the use of a narcotic drug by a patient under his care is of very little immediate importance compared with the satisfactory recovery of his patient from the condition for which he is treating him. The physician or the surgeon who has in his care a narcotic drug addict whom he is treating for another disease condition should remember that the patient's recovery from the condition for which the doctor was consulted, depends to a great extent upon the amount of functional balance and organic and metabolic adequacy which exists in that patient, and he should realize that functional balance and organic and metabolic adequacy in a narcotic addict are largely under the control of, and vary with the extent to which that patient is kept in, adequate narcotic drug balance.

The establishing and maintaining of adequate drug balance, therefore, is one of the most important elements to be considered in the conduct of a case of narcotic addiction undergoing operation or treatment for a condition other than the cure of his addiction. In handling such a patient, the physician or surgeon should completely put out of his mind any idea of at the same time trying to " cure " the addiction with which his patient is afflicted. I have repeatedly heard of many, and have personally come into contact with cases where the physician or surgeon was trying to withdraw opiate drug from a patient with addiction-disease, as an incidental in the course of treatment of other disease conditions. There are cases of addiction-disease in which this may be successfully accomplished. In the majority of cases, however, this procedure is too harmful to be anything but condemned. Not only will the surgeon or physician ordinarily fail in his attempt to remedy the addiction condition, but he may very severely handicap his other work on that patient and very seriously jeopardize the success of his efforts in the remedy of the condition which he was originally called upon to treat.

It must be remembered that addiction-disease is a chronic condition, and that it is practically never indicated as a matter of clinical emergency, in a case of established addiction, that the opiate be immediately withdrawn. As has been previously stated, drug withdrawal is very much like an operation of election to be done when the patient is ready for it and by whatever procedure is indicated when the proper time arrives. The getting of the patient ready for it often determines, just as is the case in the operation of election, to a great measure, the success of the work and the freedom from complications and sequelae.

Since the final withdrawal of drug is to be regarded as comparable to an operation of election, and the best time for its execution is a matter of arrangement and of preceding preparation, it is obvious that it should not be undertaken with expectation of satisfactory issue in the course of treatment for an ailment or condition which demands and expends much physical resistance and recuperative powers. Recuperative forces should be maintained and directed towards whatever is the indication of paramount importance at any given time. In the conduct of a surgical case or a serious medical case, the indication of paramount importance is recovery from the condition for which the patient applies to the surgeon or physician. All other conditions present should be handled in such a way as to interfere as little as possible with the successful accomplishment of the main issue. The proper control of narcotic addiction-disease mechanism and of its influences upon the patient addicted is the important problem presented by narcotic addiction as met in the field complicating surgical and general medical conditions.

CHAPTER VIII

THE first general appreciation of the widespread existence of narcotic drug use was brought about by the passage of anti-narcotic laws. The United States Federal legislation which went into effect in 1914, was what is known as the Harrison Law, still in effect and in its purpose and drafting a wise piece of legislation. It sought to limit and control the use of opiate drugs and cocaine by making their possession and distribution illegal by other than those of professional and other status designated in the law, as qualified for their intelligent application and responsible distribution. Its administration was placed in the Department of Internal Revenue under a provision which licensed responsible distributors and required a yearly tax.

Taken as a whole, in its original form, administered with understanding of addiction-disease facts, and with honest and intelligent scientific, educational and remedial activities coincidently pursued, it should be sufficient to control a rapidly growing menace. In its attitude towards the medical profession it wisely limited its restrictions to the broad statement that these drugs named must not be distributed other than in the " course of legitimate professional practice," wisely making no attempt to define such " legitimate practice," but apparently anticipating investigative activities of the scientific professions in the determination and dissemination of medical facts for the guidance of honest practitioners, and of those who should interpret and enforce the law.

Unfortunately addiction as a disease was, at that time, not a matter of wide recognition, the public in general and the medical profession itself still almost universally holding to the old conceptions of it on the basis of supposed morbid indulgence and " habit." It seems to the author that the failure of the Harrison Law to check or limit the illegitimate use of the drugs it describes, is not due to a defect in the law itself, but is due to the failure of the scientific professions to clarify the situation with a clean cut understanding of the condition legislated against. The reaction within the medical profession as a result of this law was unfortunate. Instead of stimulating scientific interest and investigation into the character of this disease, the result was that medical men in general having little or no conception of its disease basis, regarded the narcotic addict as a mental or correctional problem and left his consideration and handling to the lay officials and the special institutions whose activities had been along other lines than scientific research into physical disease.

In the minds of most lay and of many medical workers the only consideration was the stopping of drug use *per se,* an attitude which to a less extent still persists. Uninformed as to the now established facts of addiction-disease, the administrators of the law, and to a large extent the medical profession, tended to regard supply of opiate to an addict as the prolongation of a habit, and not as medication indicated by the mechanism and symptomatology of a disease — and therefore as not being legitimate medical practice. This attitude had the effect of making the practitioner of medicine unwilling to receive the narcotic addict as a patient.

The immediate result was the sudden deprivation of opiate to such addiction-disease sufferers as had not had financial means or foresight to purchase large reserves before the laws went into effect. The history of the drastic early enforcement of the various laws, reduplicated with more or less completeness by periodical legislative and administrative activities, without adequate arrangement for the relief of the narcotic-deprived addiction-disease sufferer, shows suicides and deaths, and a rapid development of exploitation of the needs of the addict at the hands of illicit commerce. For this illicit commerce the laws themselves, however, are not so much to be blamed as the influence of long-prevailing and widely-taught attitudes and conceptions which caused scientific and other forces to fail to recognize and meet the need for clinical handling of the situation, and for study and investigation of the condition. Legislators and administrators simply reflect prevailing theories.

Early theories took scant if any account of the possibilities presented by the now rapidly-growing disease conception of addiction. The popular conception of an addict and even the description met in standard medical text-books was that of a " dope-fiend," an irresponsible panderer to a morbid " habit," bereft of will-power, honor and decency, a menace to himself and to society, and this conception has had unfortunate influence in the making, interpretation, and administration of laws. That it can be truthfully applied to some people who have developed addiction-disease is unquestioned, but that it fails to take into consideration a much larger number who are not irresponsible panderers to morbid habit, nor bereft of will-power, honor and decency, nor a menace to themselves or to society, but are honest and upright members of society and economic assets in the community, accounts in large part for the failure of laws and their administration to remedy the narcotic drug situation. Measures which might be very useful in the forcible control of those who can be justly characterized as " dope fiends " work great harm to those who are simply sick people.

That these sick people have been commonly regarded

and classed as " dope-fiends " was due to the fact that the points of view and special experiences of the psychologist or psychiatrist, sociologist or penologist and the exponents of special methods of treatment dominated the literature and teaching in which appeared practically nothing of essential pathology, symptomatology and broad principles of addiction-disease therapeutics and handling. The occasional voice of the clinical student or experimental laboratory worker was almost unheard, and the opposition accorded unorthodox views and announcements made him a brave man who would state them, and tended to cause him to be regarded as an academic theorist, or possessed of ulterior motives.

In such a situation the dominant theme has been the stamping out of so-called " drug use." The physician who under his best and honest therapeutic judgment strove to meet the immediate indications of the worthy and innocent addiction-disease sufferer by the administration of opiate drug, incurred a danger of severe criticism and at times of jeopardy to his liberties under the interpretation of his acts as perpetuating a " habit."

It cannot be denied that in some cases unscrupulous holders of medical degrees have availed themselves of existing conditions in such a way that their supplying of opiates to narcotic addicts constitutes simply traffic in narcotic drugs and not the intelligent practice of medicine. It should be a matter of serious consideration for our lawmakers, administrators and judiciary, however, as to what extent the performance of the occasional medical vampire should be made a basis for the legal or administrative control of the honest practitioner, and to what extent he should be enveloped by legal and administrative restrictions, the innocent and unconscious violation of whose technicalities may at any time be made a basis for criminal procedure. It should be remembered that zealous administrators may not have proper conception of the scientific facts of disease nor of the practical problems of legitimate medical practice in addiction-disease. The quality of the act in the determination of legitimate medical practice is often if not as a rule more important than the mere act itself. There has been as yet, so far as I know, no satisfactory legal definition of legitimate medical practice. The author sees no reason why the same rules and criteria as have developed or are formulated for legitimate medical practice in other diseases might not be applied to the treatment of addiction-disease. In a general way the legitimate practice of medicine in the care of, handling of or treatment of a disease consists of such medical attention, advice, instruction and guidance, and clinical or therapeutic ministrations as may be indicated by the needs of the individual case. In addiction-disease if a physician proceeds upon the physical, clinical and other indications exhibited in the individual case, being held responsible for reasonable familiarity with such indications, and fulfilling to the best of his available equipment and professional ability the general and therapeutic requirements of each case, it is difficult for the author to see how he can be held to be engaged in illegitimate practice. He can of course be held responsible for reasonable familiarity with available teaching and information on the subject treated by him, and for average intelligence and honest application of medical principles and practice. It seems to the author that legitimate practice as determined in other diseases would go a long way towards the elimination of the charlatan and shyster physician and would not carry with it the menace and jeopardy which technical violation of often medically impractical administrative demands may involve. If the honest physician is left no leeway for the exercise of medical judgment in the handling of widely differing cases of addiction-disease, or if his exercise of honest clinical judgment is to be constantly influenced by a necessity of worrying about its possible interpretation, in the light of unduly stringent laws and regulations, a condition is created in which the intelligent practice of medicine upon the sufferer from addiction-disease becomes impossible.

' A matter about which there has been a great deal of dispute is that of the prescribing or dispensing by the practitioner of medicine of opiate drugs to the narcotic addict in the handling of narcotic addiction, itself. The adherents of the older theory of addiction being merely habit or vicious indulgence, oppose as illegitimate practice the continued supply of the opiate to an addiction patient, unless in some cases the patient also suffers from some painful and incurable disease.

They take the attitude that, if the addict did not want to keep on using opiate he would go somewhere and be cured, and that as long as he can get opiate drug he will not get " cured." The possibilities of immediate so-called " cure " are discussed elsewhere in this volume. Sufficient for present statement is the fact that, as demonstrated by the testimony of the Whitney Committee Legislative Investigation hearings, one of the most complete and valuable pieces of public investigation work into addiction ever done, there exists at present practically no adequate or competent machinery for the successful so-called " cure " of the great numbers of narcotic addicts. This is discussed elsewhere. Those who talk casually of the enforced immediate cure of the narcotic addict would do well to investigate and realize the lack of possibilities of its immediate attainment on any large scale. This is a basic fact which has been too little taken into account by those who still hold to the appetite and habit theories.

In the narcotic drug situation we are confronted by fact and not by theory. Intelligent comprehension and unbiased investigation are needed far more than we need premature conclusions drawn from insufficient experience or too narrow observation along special lines. The fundamental fact is this, as has been repeatedly stated, that the narcotic addict, until his disease mechanism can be competently and successfully arrested physically, needs the daily administration of sufficient quantities of the drug of his addiction to meet the indications of his disease. If the drug is not administered to him in sufficient amounts to meet these disease indications, he cannot be blamed if, in the agony of his suffering and the desperateness of his plight, he is forced into the underworld and the illicit channels of supply for the continuance of a physically endurable and economically possible existence. Until the medical profession and the medical institutions — hospital and otherwise — have in competent execution methods of handling and treatment of the narcotic addict which are more humane and more effective than those shown by ample testimony to be in common use, the supply of narcotic drug to the responsible narcotic addict to the extent of physical need, without unjustifiable exploitation, financial or otherwise, is the duty of the medical man. Any law which to this extent limits the supply of opiate drug to the addict should receive the support of the medical profession. Any law which renders it difficult or impossible for a physician to conscientiously and rationally meet, to this extent, the indications of narcotic drug disease, should meet from the medical profession with a united and honest attempt at its modification.

Above all there should be fostered and promoted by the medical profession an intelligent, unbiased investigation into the actual facts surrounding the problem of narcotic drug addiction as a definite disease. Such information concerning the physical and clinical facts of this disease, as we should be in a position to give, would be eagerly welcomed by the law-makers and the administrators and the judiciary; and we should be in a position to co-operate with them in the making and interpreting of narcotic drug laws. Lack of such information has played an important part in whatever mistakes our police, legislative and administrative bodies have made, and forced them to proceed as best they could to meet the demand of a public menace that could no longer be denied.

What has the law done for the addict? Like the physicians, the legislators have done the best they could in the light of their knowledge, experience and teaching. Some of them seem, however, to have had their attention directed unduly to a special class of those addicted, the addicts found among the type of person which begins or tends to end among the criminal or vicious of the so-called "underworld." Legislators and administrators have realized that the taking of narcotic drugs was rapidly spreading, and that it constituted a public menace in the class to which their attention was directed; and they applied the means at their disposal in the remedy of what they saw. But again, like the physician, they tended to center their attention upon the mere taking of narcotic drug, and they attempted to control by legislation the possession and use of narcotic drugs with too little appreciation of fundamental disease facts and of general basic considerations of widespread application. They did not seem to have appreciated the extent to which their legislation or administration would affect the great numbers of upright, and innocent and worthy addiction-sufferers of whom they did not know, and who did not possess the fundamental characteristics of the class and type of person addicted against which they legislated. They rightly directed their attention towards the control of the sources of drug supply and they rightly limited the ultimate legal supplying of drug to duly licensed and responsible persons and institutions, specifically described. The slogan of most of the special legislation has been to place responsibility for the supply and use of narcotic drugs squarely upon the shoulders of the medical profession. Such effort is wise, and this is where the responsibility belongs.   And this is where the medical profession would have it placed in so far as the medical profession supplies narcotic drugs.

The honest physician has no desire to dodge responsibility for his handling of narcotic addicts to the best of his ability, nor should he have any objection to a reasonable responsibility and accounting for narcotic drugs used in that handling; especially since the taking of narcotic drugs has in certain of its phases, developed as a serious situation entirely outside of the medical profession, in which situation these drugs are non-professionally supplied and used to such an extent as to constitute a public menace.   The non-medical supplying and administering of such drugs should not, however, be controlled in such a way as to unduly hamper their honest and legitimate use by medical men, and to deprive the honest, worthy and innocent sufferer from addiction-disease of their legitimate therapeutic administration.

One of the chief and most serious phases of the narcotic drug problem, which for obvious reasons has especially called for legislation, is the illicit and illegitimate commerce in narcotic drugs.   The class of addicts which constitutes a public menace is largely so supplied.   This fact is recognized in the recent report of the Special Committee of Investigation Appointed by the Secretary of the Treasury, in which is stated, " This illegitimate traffic has developed to enormous proportions in recent years, and is a serious menace at the present time.   It is through these channels that the addict of the underworld now secures the bulk of his supplies."

This Report further states that " there is the so-called ' underground ' traffic which is estimated to be equal in magnitude to that carried on through legitimate channels. This trade is in the hands of the so-called ' Dope peddlers,' who appear to have a national organization for procuring and disposing of their supplies.   For the most part it is thought that they obtain their supplies by smuggling them from Mexico or Canada, although smaller quantities of these drugs are obtained from unscrupulous dealers in this country or by theft," etc. There should be some way to dissociate entirely, conclusively and finally in the minds of the public the illegitimate and underworld traffic in narcotic drugs from the efforts of the honest physician to practice rational and scientific medicine in the help of the worthy and deserving addict. The regulation of the narcotic drug traffic of the underworld or "underground" is not the business of the medical profession, and the burden of responsibility for it should not be placed upon the shoulders of the medical profession or the consequences of it made to react upon the head of the honest physician and innocent addiction sufferer. There is a tremendous number of excellent and worthy and even illustrious people in whom addiction is in no way associated with vice, or other morbidity of mental or environmental origin, who are merely, solely and simply sick people suffering from addiction-disease, whose problem is the control of that disease until it can be arrested by competent therapeutic procedure, for which they constantly seek. Misconception of them and neglect of sufficient consideration of them is the tragic aspect of the narcotic drug situation, and causes tremendous individual and economic wastage. They do not in any way associate with underground traffic unless or until driven to it by failure of legitimate sources of opiate medication, or by the surrounding of legitimate sources with such restrictions as make the man of standing and reputation, afflicted with addiction-disease, fear possible publicity and economic detriment.

It is the duty of the medical organizations to see to it that these deserving purely medical problems and worthy sick people and their honest medical advisers shall no longer than avoidable be permitted to remain confused in the minds of the laity and of the medical profession itself with the problems of regulation of " underground " traffic and the control of the " underworld " addict. It is the duty of the medical organizations also to see to it that in the public press and elsewhere, and especially in their own scientific journals, the acts of the occasional individual with medical degree who prostitutes his medical standing and the aims and ideals of his profession in the commercial exploitation of the drug addict are not presented in such a way as to cause by inference or otherwise, their confusion with the honest efforts of honest medical men who are engaged to the best of their ability in the humane and ethical help of the deserving sufferer from addiction-disease.

It is, furthermore, the duty of the medical organizations to see to it that whatever laws and regulations are promulgated in the control of criminal and unworthy shall not be framed or administered in such a way as to unnecessarily jeopardize the reputation and liberties of the honest practitioner and to interfere with his conscientious efforts to care for his honest and innocent addiction-disease patients to such an extent as makes that care impossible.

Legislation or administrative regulation which limits to responsible and authorized persons possession and distribution of narcotic drugs and which compels from such persons reasonable accounting for such possession and distribution, is under conditions which have long existed but only recently been sufficiently recognized necessary and desirable. The Harrison Law was a definite response to an obvious need, in its obvious intent and draughting a wise and unobjectionable legislation. It provided for responsible possession and distribution and it enforced an accounting for the same, but did not unwisely restrict, in its text, nor hamper the legitimate possession and honest therapeutic employment of narcotic drugs. From the medical organizations and educational and scientific institutions should be available scientific study and understanding of narcotic drug addiction-disease available for the information of conscientious executives and administrators, who must exercise their best judgment in the light of available and prevailing teaching. It is the duty of the medical organizations to see to it that available and prevailing addiction-disease information and teaching is honest, unbiased and competent.

Those who are responsible for our laws should remember that the possible interpretation and administration of the laws they draught are very important considerations, and determine the real effect of the laws often more than does the intent of the makers. Legislation which is unduly stringent or is capable of unduly stringent administration may have unfortunate reaction and influence upon honest effort in the care of the deserving sick. Restricting beyond reasonable limits the care of the honest narcotic drug addict simply tends to make it impracticable and dangerous for the average medical man to have anything to do with narcotic addicts, and to drive the honest and deserving patient into the underworld, into the insane asylum or to suicide. Until we have provided scientific and clinical study, and have thoroughly investigated present and possible medical treatment and handling of narcotic-drug addiction-disease, and have established humane and effective therapeutic measures and procedures in the control and remedy of this disease, we should not deprive the majority of honest addicts of the only medication and means by which they can at present remain self-supporting citizens. The handling of the problem of the underworld and of underground supply is not going to be solved by too restrictive regulation of the honest physician. Legislation or regulation which makes it practically impossible for the honest physician to care for the honest case of addiction-disease is a boon to charlatans, and medical shysters, and the illicit underworld traffic.

It is the opinion of some that the handling and treatment of narcotic addiction should be taken out of the hands of the practitioner of medicine. The statement is made that the practitioner of medicine is not competent to handle a case of this disease. It has been advised that the treatment of narcotic addicts should be restricted to a small number of specially designated and licensed men and institutions. How and by whom are those special men and institutions to be selected? In the present state of chaotic and widely diversified medical and lay opinion as to narcotic addiction and the narcotic addict it would be a very difficult matter to select the men or the institutions for such absolute control. The comprehension, study and investigation of narcotic drug addiction has entered a stage of evolution and development in which new facts and new truths — both as to the addict and as to the condition from which he suffers — are being recognized and must be threshed out, correlated and coordinated with hitherto existing opinion before too restrictive measures will be anything but narrow-visioned, premature and harmful.

There are undoubtedly institutions, many of them not widely known, in which is available skillful, humane, intelligent and successful handling of this disease. From personal observation and experience in institutional work, and from analysis and investigation of many histories, it is my opinion that the results of institutional treatment depend more upon the quality of its medical and nursing staff than upon any other consideration. That the mere fact that addiction-disease is handled in an institution is a very minor consideration in comparison with the intelligence of that handling, is amply attested to in the testimony of the Whitney Hearings and by the experience of many addicts. Unquestionably, unknown and large numbers of narcotic addicts have been relieved of their addiction in reputable sanitaria conducted by skillful and competent medical men.   Also unquestionably, large numbers of addicts have been relieved of their addiction through the honest efforts of practitioners of medicine, in private practice.   Unfortunately these efforts and their results have received entirely too little recognition.

The average physician may be inexpert and not as completely educated in the appreciation, understanding and clinical handling of narcotic drug addiction-disease as he is in other diseases.   The common-sense remedy for this situation, however, is not to drive the addict out of his hands, but to make him as competent in that addict's handling as he is in any other clinical condition.   It is only a matter of time and education before the competent practitioner of internal medicine can be brought to a comprehension of and ability to intelligently handle addiction-disease.   It is largely a matter of securing general appreciation of and ability to clinically recognize, and interpret physical symptomatology, and to meet the indications of individual disease manifestations.

The ultimate solution of the problem of handling the narcotic addict lies largely in the education of medical men, both in institutions and in private practice, and through them securing lay appreciation of disease facts. Any legal or administrative restrictions which drive the care of the honest addict out of the hands of the honest medical man simply postpone the day when this ideal may be consummated.

Some addicts, as individuals and types, will of course always require institutional and custodial handling.   The handling of the addict who is criminal or vicious belongs within the province of the penological authorities, just as does the handling of any other man who is criminal or vicious.   The handling of the addict who is fundamentally degenerate, defective or mentally weak may require the attention of the alienist and institutional restraint, just as may the handling of any other man who is degenerate or defective. Narcotic drug addiction-disease in the man who is vicious or criminal or defective or degenerate should be treated as narcotic drug addiction-disease, as any other disease is treated in the same individual.

To our legislators and administrators and forces of penology, custody and correction rightfully belongs the problem of looking after the criminal and vicious addict as well as providing for the eradication of illicit, irresponsible, and "underground" traffic in narcotic drugs. If the illicit trafficker happens to be a physician he should have no more consideration at the hands of the law than any other criminal and in its action the law should have complete co-operation of the medical profession, which should see to it also that conscientious endeavor of its honest members is not confused in its consideration with illicit traffic and that the acts of the doctor shall be determined and estimated upon broad principles of medical practice and not upon violation of incidental technicalities. Great care should be taken that the sins of a guilty few are not visited upon the heads of a deserving many.

Until there is available competent and adequate medical care for the honest narcotic addict sufficient in extent to meet the needs of the thousands of sufferers, and encouragement and protection as well as restriction is afforded to the honest physician, the illicit traffic will continue and grow, including in its toils many who would not otherwise seek it. Before we have further medical restrictions, we should have both medical and lay and official education. Over-emphasis on any aspect resulting in premature, narrow, ill-considered and ill-advised action only increases the complexity of the situation and defers final remedy. For as great and complicated a problem as narcotic drug addiction there will be found no special or specific panacea.

In conclusion I feel that a great deal more thought and attention should be paid to the testimony of the public hearings of the New York Legislative Investigating Committee, under the leadership of Senator George H. Whitney, Chairman of the Committee. A vast amount of valuable data was produced. It showed for the first time to my knowledge an official effort to secure the true story of the narcotic addict in all of its applications and circumstances. It is significant that the Preliminary Report of the Whitney Committee gave official recognition of the fact that narcotic drug addiction is a physical disease. So important and enlightening was the above mentioned report, that it is deemed desirable to quote from it in part as follows:

" Lack of understanding and appreciation of the disease of narcotic drug addiction and its treatment by a large majority of the medical profession has fostered conditions which make it impossible to determine a rational procedure for treating and curing the addicted by the State at this time.

" Such absence of uniformity of opinion has worked great hardship upon the public and has laid the narcotic drug addict open to misconception, misunderstanding and medical treatment which, in many instances, has resulted in harm rather than good.

" Evidence offered by physicians shows that many addicts have died under the methods of treatment existing to-day and that a large percentage of those discharged from institutions as ' cured ' are driven back to use of narcotics through unbearable physical torture induced by improper withdrawal of their drug.

" Evidence from physicians was adduced which denied that any cure for narcotic drug addiction existed in any of the private or public institutions of this State. Evidence from other eminent physicians was adduced which bore testimony to the fact that the disease of narcotic drug addiction was curable.

" The difference of medical opinion existing in medical circles regarding this vitally important question should be made the subject of a thorough and searching investigation as a matter of the greatest importance to the welfare of a large number of people in the State of New York.

" Your Committee has found that narcotic drug addiction bears no relation in point of character and seriousness to any other known habit induced by the use of stimulants. Narcotic drug addicts, according to evidence adduced, should not be classed with the alcoholic or the tobacco addict or the cocaine habitue.

" The constant use of narcotics produces a condition in the human body that many physicians of medical authority now recognize as a definite disease, which diseased condition absolutely requires a continued administration of narcotics to keep the body in normal function unless proper treatment and cure is provided.

" Withdrawal of the drug of addiction induces such fundamental physical disorganization and unbearable pain that addicts are driven to any extreme to obtain narcotic drugs and allay their suffering by self-administration.

" Testimony of physicians coming in contact with the addicts and statements of addicts themselves show that those afflicted with this disease express every desire to secure humane and competent treatment and cure and that most narcotic drug users are willing to undergo physical torture and often do voluntarily undergo such torture, in an effort to be rid of their so-called habit.

" In the present chaotic condition of medical opinion on this subject, it is impossible for the addict to-day to either secure authentic information on the subject of his disease and its treatment, or to procure at the hands of the average physician competent treatment for his malady.

" It has further been stated by competent authorities before your Committee that drug addiction is not confined to the criminal or defective class of humanity.

" This disease, however contracted, is prevalent among members of every social class. Some physicians estimate that addicts of the so-called underworld are far out-numbered by unfortunate drug users drafted from social circles of refinement and intelligence in the State of New York, who have become addicted to the constant use of narcotic drugs, but who are able to hide their affliction from the public.

" The attitude of the public toward the narcotic drug addict, fostered by the increasing prevalence of the disease in the criminal classes and by the apparent lack of medical help, has forced such drug users to keep their affliction a secret.

" This necessity in turn, your Committee finds, has apparently contributed to the existence of many unsound nostrums for the cure of narcotic drug addiction and many private institutions where this disease is purported to be cured which exist solely for the purpose of preying upon the addict.

" State investigation and regulation of such cures and institutions is recommended by your Committee.

" Your Committee is inclined to criticize the medical profession for its lack of study of the increasingly important subject of narcotic drug addiction. The only excuse which can be offered for this unfortunate condition lies in the fact that there has not been medical appreciation of conditions and that legislation, both State and Federal, has forced upon the physician a situation for which he was wholly unprepared.

" The testimony taken by your Committee shows that those charged with the sale and distribution of narcotic drugs are in the main observing the law, and that the legal distribution of these drugs is less than before the enactment of existing narcotic laws, Federal and State.

" On the other hand it is apparent from this testimony that public consumption of narcotic drugs has increased to an alarming extent.   The inevitable conclusion is that the unfortunate addict has been forced to and does obtain his supply illegally.

" This condition arises very largely from the fact that many physicians and pharmacists, either through misunderstanding of the law or the true nature of the addict's disease, have refused to prescribe or dispense narcotic drugs to the sufferer.

" Your Committee contends that any member of the medical or pharmaceutical professions who refuses either to prescribe or to dispense narcotic drugs to the honest addict to alleviate the suffering and pain occasioned by lack of narcotics is not living up to the high standards of humanity and intelligence established by these great professions."

CHAPTER IX

BEFORE commenting upon the legitimate use of narcotics, it is desirable to emphasize again that the term
" narcotics " as used in this volume refers particularly to
the preparations and derivatives of opium, because as
the term " narcotics " has come to be used it is synonymous in the minds of many with " habit-forming drugs," a
phrase often loosely used and grouping under its title a
number of drugs of widely dissimilar action and properties.

Although many of these drugs have narcotic properties,
their action upon the human body is in many respects
totally unlike the action of the opiates themselves. Also
the condition resulting from their prolonged and continuous administration is an entirely different condition
clinically and physiologically from that manifested in the
case of opiate addiction-disease. The problems associated
with the use of alcohol, cocaine, chloral, cannabis, the
various coal tars, etc., differ from each other and all of
them are, in their basic medical principles, of an entirely
different character from the problems associated with the
use of opiates. As has been previously stated, it has not
yet been demonstrated that any of them form the basis
for an addiction-disease mechanism such as clinical study
and laboratory experiment seem to demonstrate in opiate
addiction-disease.

In considering legitimate as well as illegitimate use
of opiates, therefore, it is important not to confuse them
114

with the drugs above mentioned and to be sure that in the mind of the reader there shall not exist any lingering impression that attributes popularly supposed to be associated with so-called " habit-forming drugs " are of necessity displayed in the opiate group.

The habitual use of cocaine for example, may be regarded as an indulgence of appetite and the obtaining of sensation and artificial stimulation and not as based upon the demands of a specific physical addiction-disease mechanism. The therapeutics of its discontinuance are entirely different. Habitual indulgence in cocaine tends to result in mental and moral deterioration. In the addict of the so-called " underworld " it is the coincident use of cocaine with its manifestations of mental, moral and physical deterioration that has led to the wide and erroneous attributing of characteristics of this class of cocaine habituates to the average opiate addict. The habitual use of cocaine is an entirely different matter from the continued administration of opiate in the case of an opiate addict, and its manifestations should be completely dissociated from the clinical picture and problem of opiate addiction-disease.

Some writers, especially those associated with municipal or state institutions of penology and correction, lay emphasis upon the case of the so-called " mixed addict." The crimes of violence with which addiction has become associated in the popular mind are practically never connected with the action of opiate drug. They are, however, characteristic of the cocaine crazed individual. When they are performed by a so-called " mixed addict " they are the result of cocaine habituation rather than of opiate addiction. Such crimes of violence as are committed by the opium or morphine addict are well explained in the Report of the Treasury Investigation Committee in the following words, " There are many instances of cases where victims of this disease were among people of the highest qualities morally and intellectually, and of the greatest value to their communities, who, when driven by sudden deprivation of their drug, have been led to commit felony or violence to relieve their misery."

This erroneous grouping of so-called "habit forming drugs" is to some extent responsible for a misconception of opiates and of opiate use and opiate result to such an extent that there is unfortunately manifested at times a lack of appreciation of the very important legitimate uses of these drugs.

The paramount issue of legitimate narcotic medication is that of the opiates. Opiates form and must continue to form the most indispensable medication, emergency and otherwise, for shock, wounds and allied conditions. It may be safely stated that of all emergency medication, the opiates would be the last to be surrendered by the intelligent physician or surgeon. This is true of every day civil practice and its importance is increased tremendously under conditions of active warfare.

The opiates possess combined actions and powers not found in any other group of drugs. In therapeutic doses they support the heart and circulation, they relieve pain, they hold in check excessive activity of the glands of internal secretion with all their associated phenomena of exhaustion and collapse; they control spasm and they give sleep. In no other drugs or group of drugs are these properties combined as they are in the opiate group. In emergency medication, opium and its alkaloids, especially morphine, are the medications often most responsible for the saving of life and reason. It is not necessary to argue this point with any intelligent physician or surgeon. For the benefit of the laity, however, and for the benefit of the occasional fanatic and hysterical reformer it is well to state that without the use of morphine and other opiates the mortality among the sick and wounded would be vastly greater, and many of those who might survive in spite

of its non-administration to them would bear for the rest
of their lives physical and mental and nerve consequences
of gravest character.   The lives and minds that have been
saved by the timely administration of an opiate drug are
incalculable.   One has only to talk with those who have
worked under the stern necessities and emergency conditions of warfare to appreciate this fact.   There is no
known drug which will replace clinically and therapeutically the opiate group.   At present it is as indispensable
in meeting emergency indications as is the scalpel of the
surgeon.

It would be entirely unnecessary to discuss or to apparently defend the use of narcotics in peace as well as in
war-time medication if it were not for the fact of recent
recognition of the wide existence of opiate addiction in
the civilized world.   Combined with this is the belief,
often met, that as a result of prolonged opiate administration, a certain proportion of soldiers have developed
this condition.   If the facts of addiction-disease were
widely known and applied to its proper handling and
remedy, there should be no hysteria concerning and no
criticism against legitimate opiate medication; even if unavoidably continued to the point of creating this condition.   That opiate-addiction is one of the medical problems of war is recognized and must be openly met.   In
many cases, just as in private civil practice, the physician
is confronted by a choice of evils.   To save life or reason he must continue opiate medication even into and
past the danger zone of beginning opiate addiction.   Lack
of popular recognition, appreciation and comprehension of
this fact, in the present status of narcotic addiction, contains grave dangers of hysteria and of undeserved and
irresponsible criticism.   That this criticism is based on
ignorance makes it none the less unpleasant and hamper-
ing to efficient service.

It should be at once and widely taught that the cases

of opiate addiction that follow war time administration of opiate do not constitute a new medical problem, but simply constitute additional cases of a disease which has existed insufficiently appreciated in this country for over half a century. When the conditions under which wounded and sick must be handled in the emergencies of war, and the higher percentage of urgent and severe cases are taken into account, it will be found that the proportion of wounded and sick soldiers with this addiction-disease is no greater and is very probably not so great as the proportion of people in civil life and practice who have in the past contracted this disease, and are even at present contracting it as a result of opiate medication, unavoidably or otherwise continued to the point of addiction.

As the facts of addiction-disease development as a result of unavoidable military therapeutics become known it will be well to remember that the conditions are no different in character and exist in no greater relative proportion than the same conditions in civil life and practice. The principal difference lies in the greater opportunity for early recognition.

As to the illegitimate or non-therapeutic contraction of addiction within the army, its dangers are no greater and possibly not as great as in civil life. Some non-medical cases of addiction may have developed within the ranks of the army. It may be said of them, however, that army life and activity and training probably saved many more or less idle and ignorant youths imbued with a spirit of curiosity, and with lack of normal outlet for physical and nervous surplus energies, from the associations and environments which have been taken advantage of by those associated with illicit commerce in the creation of the addict of non-medical origin, which has so increased in the past four or five years.

It is my belief that the gathering together of young men presents an opportunity for the education of the youth as to the physical and disease facts of opiate addiction which should be of incalculable benefit in the solution of the narcotic problem and in the suppression and prevention of "underground" and underworld narcotic traffic.

The foregoing opens to discussion another legitimate use of narcotics. This use is the intelligent administration of opiate in the control and therapeutic handling of whatever cases of addiction are found to exist. The situation within the army as regards addiction is in the general indications for its handling, identical with the situation existing in civil life. The man who has fully developed opiate addiction-disease will have to have his opiate supplied to him intelligently and with proper appreciation of the symptomatology and reactions of addiction-disease until there is equipment and educated personnel provided for his intelligent and competent handling. Under any other immediate arrangements, the addicted soldier, just as the addicted civilian, will in his desperation and physical torments of bodily need for opiate drug, endeavor to smuggle, steal or otherwise obtain in any way possible this medication.

In brief then, and to recapitulate, the legitimate use of narcotics will be roughly divided under two broad heads. The first is the necessary administration of opiate to those who are not addicted for the control of emergency or other indication with which every competent physician or surgeon is familiar. To use opiate as indicated in such cases is not only legitimate, but failure to use it would be inhuman and barbarous and result in the loss of many lives and in the making of wrecks of many others. The second is the administration of opiates to those unfortunates, who either through their own ignorance or carelessness, or through unavoidably or otherwise prolonged legitimate or necessary medication have developed in their body the condition of opiate addiction-disease, until such time as their disease can be arrested by competent medical care of their addiction-disease mechanism.

As to addiction created in war time, there is considerable amount of information. This is not the time nor the place for detailed discussion of that information. Calm consideration of it should, however, suffice to still the voice of any objections and irrefutably answer arguments criticizing existence of war-time addiction. The greatly lacking and needed element in its consideration and handling is appreciation of it as physical, controllable and arrestable disease. The laity and the mothers and other relatives and the friends of those in the Army and Navy will not exhibit panic and fear once the intangible horror and vague and morbid and erroneous picture of the " dope fiend " is in its application to opiate addiction erased from popular conception and replaced by comprehension of a definite physical disease clinically controllable and in most cases therapeutically remediable.

To what extent narcotic drug addiction-disease will prove to be a medical sequela of war and of necessary war-time medication may never be made a matter of accurate statistics. The popular and prevailing attitudes towards and conception of the condition and of its possessor tend to influence towards desperate concealment rather than to encourage self-revelation. As has been stated before addiction-disease followed the Civil War, occasional cases recently existing and possibly still existing among the few remaining veterans of that struggle, addiction dating back to Civil War medication. The Spanish War and necessary medication added to the list of war-time contracted addiction-disease. Of addiction among those participating in the last war, it is at present wise to simply recognize the condition, and to hope that as the addiction-disease sufferer, developed through necessary war-time medication becomes known, he will not have to carry the addiction stigma of past attitudes and conceptions, and that we shall be in a position to accord him intelligent and humane consideration and handling as a deserving sick man, whose disease was contracted in our defense.

CHAPTER X

FROM the foregoing it is easy to see that the sooner the established facts of the fundamental physical basis and reactions of the addiction-states become matters of medical, sociological, administrative, and lay knowledge, the earlier there will be a rational and practical consideration of the use as well as of the abuse of narcotic drugs, and a beginning of solution of the narcotic drug problem.

Lack of knowledge of the fundamental and constant physical reactions and phenomena, and of the characteristic clinical manifestations of this disease, and of the physical suffering of drug deprivation is in a very large measure responsible for failure in its therapeutic handling in the past, and indirectly responsible for whatever is unjust and misdirected in the framing of the various laws, and also for a great part of whatever incompetency and lack of wisdom has appeared in their administration.

Lack of knowledge of the disease facts of narcotic addiction is also responsible for the practical absence of widespread provision for humane and intelligent handling, for much of the jeopardy and fear on the part of the medical practitioner towards these cases, and for the existence of conditions resulting in the rapid growth and increase of the worst evils of the present situation.

The worst evils of the narcotic drug situation are not, as is widely taught, rooted in the inherent depravity and moral weakness of those addicted. They find their origin in opportunity, created by ignorance, neglect and fear,

122

for commercial and other exploitation of the physical suffering resulting from denial of narcotic drug to one addicted. The many widely advertised drug cures derive their prosperity from the desperate desire of the narcotic addict to be cured of the condition which may at any time cause him intense physical suffering. The worst evil of the narcotic situation in the past few years, and especially since the enforcement of restrictive legislation, without provision for complete investigation of the whole situation, for education, and adequate treatment of disease aspects, is the rapid growth and spread of criminal and underworld and illicit traffic in narcotic drugs. This exists to its present extent because conditions have been created which make smuggling and street peddling and criminal and illicit traffic tremendously profitable, and it would not exist to its present extent otherwise. It is simply and plainly the exploitation of human suffering by the supplying to desperate and diseased individuals, at any price which may be demanded, one of the necessities of their immediate existence.

Such exploitation would become unprofitable on any large scale if the disease created by continued administration of opiates were recognized as it exists and its physical demands comprehended and provided for in more legitimate and less objectionable ways.

One of the most important and immediately available of these ways is the honest practitioner of medicine. If the average practitioner of medicine were made familiar with the physical facts of addiction-disease, and its phenomena and reactions, and were encouraged by both legal and medical authoritative support to admit addiction-disease patients to his practice, to be cared for just as other patients to the best of his honest therapeutic ability and judgment — if he were taught to regard them as sick people whom he could help — if he were relieved of uncertainty as to the meaning and possible interpretation of laws and regulations, and as to the possible action or lack of action and attitude of his medical brethren and medical organizations towards him — the best available, honest, humane and intelligent machinery would be set in motion for the immediate care of the average honest sufferer from addiction-disease, and for the discouragement of underworld or underground exploitation. This has been demonstrated. It would react furthermore as a stimulus to the education of the physician, to familiarize himself with the scientific and medical facts of this disease.

Another immediate provision is the establishing under proper supervision and management, especially as to competent medical management, and without possibilities of humiliation and interference with self-support, of stations or clinics at which those who for financial or other reasons are unable to secure reputable and honest medical help, may obtain their necessary opiate at minimum expense and in physically necessary amounts to enable them to work and support themselves and families, without resorting to underworld associations and illicit commerce. Such clinics might be established in connection with the various hospitals on the same basis as their other medical and surgical clinics or dispensaries, and in connection with various health departments. In them the narcotic addict could not only be supplied with opiate medication, but taught the nature of his disease and the elements and principles of its control and be given such medication other than opiate for the relief of such associated or intercurrent conditions as might exist. Such clinics would have great educational value, as well as fulfilling a therapeutic need.

Pending further study and investigation and education into narcotic drug addiction-disease and the conditions surrounding it, and pending the widespread acceptance and recognition of practical and desirable procedures in the handling of the disease, and pending the provision of sufficient and scientifically adequate accommodations for the army of those who seek relief — legitimate supply of the drug of addiction under medically competent and intelligent direction fulfills a great economic and sociologic and medical need.

The financial possibilities of commercial exploitation of the sufferings of addiction-disease, combined with general ignorance of the true nature of the addiction condition, are responsible for the tremendous increase of late of narcotic addiction, of non-medical or non-therapeutic origin, among the youth. In ignorance of actual physical results, not knowing nor ever having been told that they are contracting a disease of torturing manifestations, actuated by curiosity and search for adventure, in some cases stimulated by unfortunate spectacular publicity, the youths fell easy prey to the agents, male and female, of the drug trafficker. The trafficker's intended consummation is reached when these youths finally become, to their surprise and consternation, through the development of addiction-disease and physical dependence upon narcotic drug, enforced and continued customers and in some cases, virtual slaves.

Those who are interested in prostitution and in so-called " white-slavery " would do well to turn their attention to the chains forged by the suffering, and the fear of suffering, experienced by those who have developed narcotic drug addiction-disease.

It is this class of youthful addicts that has so alarmingly increased since the enforcement of the various narcotic laws. I have previously called attention to this situation, and also to the fact that for this increase the laws themselves are not so much to be blamed as is the totally inadequate meeting of the clinical and therapeutic and educational needs of the narcotic drug situation. There has been practically no organized scientific, medical or public health activity, so far as I know, directed towards the clinical and laboratory investigation of this disease — towards a dispassionate review, analysis and testing out of the truths and errors of its literature — towards an investigation of the scientific and other qualifications and experience of those whose utterances or writings influence medical and lay opinion and action, towards the establishing of pathological and physical facts and reactions and of clinical symptomatology and phenomena as fundamental bases for its rational handling and therapeutics, and for practical education of the public as to its sufferings and dangers.

The neglect of this education is largely indirectly responsible for illicit traffic in narcotic drugs. Illicit and underground traffic exists because it is profitable. This is the direct and immediate reason for its existence. Every new addict made of an adventurous youth means a new customer for the smugglers and vendors. If that adventurous youth had been taught the facts of the physical hell of the " withdrawal signs " of opiate addiction-disease — if he knew the sufferings attendant upon body-need for opiate drug — if he knew that any red-blooded animal will develop this physical body need if opiate drug is administered for a sufficiently prolonged period — that no living being is immune to the development of this disease — if he thought of addiction as he thinks of tuberculosis, and as he is now being taught to regard venereal-disease, instead of it as being something vague and surrounded by a halo of adventure and experience, he would not fall an easy victim to the agents of the trafficker. In other words, the most potent activity in the arrest of development of even the vicious and criminal aspects of the narcotic addiction situation lies in education. Laws and their enforcement in the control of the incorrigible and vicious will always be a necessity, but laws and their administration alone are not sufficient for the control of the many-sided addiction situation. Even in the control

of smuggling and illicit traffic we need the application
of every available influence capable of exertion, not only
upon its end results but upon the machinery of its origin
and development. As so much of it originates and develops through ignorance, the method of its remedy lies
in education, education as to the facts of narcotic drug
addiction-disease.

It is ignorance also that has stamped the honest and
innocent, worthy and intelligent, and often illustrious
sufferer from narcotic addiction-disease with the attributes
and characteristics of the inherently irresponsible or otherwise incapable of self-guidance and self-restraint. The
ignorance of the facts of addiction-disease has taken from
these people even their ordinary legal and public rights
in any issue which involved the possible revelation of
their addiction. It has placed them in a position where
any procedure which might reveal their narcotic medication would expose them to public gaze as members of a
popularly despised and unworthy class of individuals.
Until very recently the testimony of a known narcotic
addict has been almost as a rule of no value in a court
of law. Irrespective of a life-time of honesty and accomplishment, the revelation of a minute might destroy the
reputation and standing of many years. Whatever the
injustices or grievances suffered by an addict, he could
not hope to evoke the protection or rights accorded an
ordinary individual under statute law without the practical certainty, if his addiction became revealed, of personal, social and economic detriment far in excess of the
legal rights to which he was entitled. The continuation
of whatever is spurious or unworthy in methods of handling, advertised or otherwise, lies partly in the fact that
the former patient cannot afford, however great his physical or other damage, to make public the existence of
addiction-disease by the instituting of a suit for malprac-
tice or other civil or criminal procedure. This alone has

been one of the factors in lack of progress and in the persistence of narrow vision or false conception. He is in effect, however high his personal, moral and other status, deprived of some of his constitutional rights, simply because he has developed addiction-disease.

The great numbers of innocent and worthy unsuspected sufferers from this disease, who could not by any stretch of wildest imagination, be regarded as mentally or morally abnormal or subnormal have therefore been placed in a position where they could not afford to demand their rights or state their case. Their problems are only recently beginning to receive general consideration. Their cases have compelled us to revise our conception of the narcotic addict, and to question ourselves as to the necessity for their continued addiction over the years of their addiction. For their own good and that of society, what shall we do with them, and what can we do for them? In the present state of public opinion and public attitude towards narcotic addicts in general would it benefit either them or society to class them merely as " drug addicts " along with the drug-users of other types of individuals and other personal characteristics for administrative handling by detailed administrative supervision and control? Can the same administrative and other methods which admittedly must be employed to protect society from the manifestly unfit accomplish anything of good in the cases of these responsible and valuable citizens?

Until there is a truer understanding of addiction-disease, and a wider appreciation of the facts that the personal attributes of its victims differ as widely as those of cardiac or any other disease condition, and that merely because a man has contracted this disease is no reason for regarding him as in any way unworthy or unfit — will stringent and drastic forcible regulative measures directed against mere use of narcotics work out to the advancement or hindrance of ultimate solution and to the ultimate benefit or harm of society? These are the questions to be applied to all restrictive administrative activities. The problem of the care of the worthy and innocent addict in such a way as not to unnecessarily harm him nor deprive his family and society of his competent activity is just as important as the handling of the addict of the type of individual from whom society must be protected. The large numbers of worthy and valued citizens who are individually and personally social and economic assets and who are sufferers from addiction-disease constitute a very important consideration in the narcotic problem.

They certainly are not fit subjects for enforced custodial and correctional handling, and if such were forced upon them they would be seriously harmed, personally, socially, economically and physically. Very many of them our equals or betters, we have no right to subject them to associations and experiences which we ourselves would rebel against and be humiliated by simply because they have developed a disease condition from which no one of us is immune.

Where is the blame for their continued addiction? Certainly not because of lack of effort on their part. Addicted for years, they have tried one after another of the various and diverse treatments and so-called cures without success or benefit. Is the blame theirs for lack of success and cure, or has there been something wrong in our treatment and handling of them? Did we know enough about addiction-disease to treat them intelligently and to exercise upon their cases the same professional skill and technical ability that we have been educated and trained to apply to other diseases? In the light of present available clinical information and study, and in the light of recent and competent laboratory research, we are forced to admit that we have not treated our addiction sufferers with sympathetic understanding and clinical competency, and that the blame for past failure to control the narcotic drug problem rests largely upon the educational inadequacy of the past.

We are in a stage of transition in our concepts of, attitude towards, and handling of the narcotic addict. Serious consideration of drug addiction as a problem of clinical and internal medicine, and of experimental laboratory research is a comparatively new thing to a majority of the medical profession, and of course also to legislators and administrators. We should all remember that no matter how strong we are in our beliefs and theories, there are many others whose experiences and results have caused them to hold just as strongly to opposite theories and beliefs, and that we are all on trial for the validity and extent of practical application of our beliefs and theories.

Each new theory or belief that is brought forward should be taken simply for record and investigation. Much that we believe to-day we know to-morrow to be based upon misinterpretation and lack of complete information. Much that we believed in the past to apply to and solve conditions, we found later to have been merely based upon observations of distracting incidentals or non-basic aspects and phases. What we need is competent, disinterested, and honest effort to get together and evaluate all available material of whatever sort and from whatever source. If it were possible of accomplishment, it would be of advantage to get together in open and frequent discussion the various workers in the field. We are all partly wrong and partly right. There is no one of us who cannot learn from any one of the others. The real end of effort should be, not to prove one or another of us right, but to take each from the other whatever is of value and all to contribute in true scientific spirit of broad tolerance towards the ideas of others and of willingness to correct or modify ideas and theories of our own, searching for no panaceas or specifics, medical, legislative or administrative, simply hunting for truth wherever we may find it and applying it intelligently to meet the needs of the individual.

There is too much work to be done, and the situation is too urgent for remedy, to permit of longer delay in scientific approach. Under present conditions, no man's announcement of theory or of remedy is to be taken as ultimate authority, but simply as his opinion based on his personal deductions, and his personal experience, to be evaluated in accordance with the extent and variety of his personal experience in the light of his individual ability and training.

Education and training are the best hopes we have as a foundation for the alleviation of present conditions and the prevention of their further spread. Lack of appreciation of and of ability to recognize and meet varied and various clinical and other indications for treatment and handling under widely different circumstances and in widely differing individuals means failure in a majority of cases, and throws a burden upon society and a complexity of problems upon municipal, state and federal authorities which they are unable to meet. Each class of workers should be working in its own field in co-operation with those working in other fields, none trying to dominate the rest, but each giving to the others credit for honest effort and appreciation of difficulties to be made easier if possible.

All possible forces should be encouraged to the work of study and investigation and education. A campaign of medical and lay investigation and education will require a much shorter time than a continuous trying out of various panaceas, medical, legislative or administrative. Also, it will bring far more satisfactory and earlier results. The narcotic wards of our great charity hospitals should be made use of for honest unbiased and trained clinical and laboratory study. The narcotic addict himself should be given a much wider hearing than he has in the past received. The mass of honest and intelligent narcotic addicts should be encouraged to tell their stories and their experiences, and should receive a fair and unbiased hearing as to the reactions upon them of various measures proposed. We, doctors, legislators, administrators are in truth as much on trial with the narcotic addict and with society for our understanding and handling of the narcotic addict and his problems as the addict is for his condition.

The remedy is plain, and the necessity for immediate activity is obvious. Education — scientific medical and lay, administrative and public health education is the lacking element or factor in the solution of the many sided narcotic drug problem. Appreciation of addiction-disease and what it may mean in the individual should be as widespread and as comprehensive as possible and at the earliest possible moment.

Without a basis of generally recognized and widely appreciated fundamental facts, there can be no competent treatment, legislation, administration or judicial decision. There can be no competent evaluation of the merits and defects of various measures promulgated, medical, legislative or administrative. There can be no competent selection of those in whose hands shall lie the handling of a tremendous problem, a problem of disease, of sociology, of economics, of public health and welfare. There can be no competent evaluation of the remedies advanced, nor of the qualifications and true authority of those who recommend them. Under such conditions various measures or procedures in their adoption or discarding or application must depend more upon the publicity and other influence of their proponents than upon their intrinsic values.

There are always some things about any condition which either are or are not, some things which are physically determinable. The basic facts of addiction-disease are now physically determinable. There are many material and obvious and easily demonstrable physical facts of greatest value to the medical profession and to the laity, facts which are still but little appreciated, and not widely known.

These facts in addiction-disease could be easily investigated. The various conflicting statements of different schools of thought or of observers working from different angles should be investigated, evaluated and correlated — taking from each whatever is useful, determining its true sphere of application and making it available to all. Every possible interest or worker should be encouraged, and every source of information sought out, not least among them the honest and intelligent sufferer from addiction-disease of many years duration whose knowledge of the facts of his condition, and efforts to control it, and search for and trial of remedy and remedies for it, and the experiences and problems, social, economic and personal, which its possession has forced upon him would constitute a touchstone of greatest value for the determination of validity of promulgated measures and procedures.

The wards of the great charity hospitals, the institutions of science and medical experiment and research, the Departments of Health, and the Public Health Services are in existence and are equipped for the early determination of clinical, and laboratory facts, and for their dissemination. These are the things towards which their activities are directed in other diseases and conditions affecting public welfare and public health. It would take a very short time to determine the physical facts of addiction-disease — to establish finally and conclusively its clinical symptomatology and constant reactions and phenomena for authoritative and educational dissemination. Every one of us who has written in description or exposition of his study and observations, together with what we have written and taught, should be made the subject of critical and unbiased investigation, and whatever of truth we have stated should be made the possession of all. The experimental development of addiction-disease in dogs and other experimental laboratory animals, the symptoms and phenomena observed in them recorded by instruments such as the sphygmomanometer and the sphygmograph and paralleling similar records and observations upon the addicted human, the reactions of the serum of these animals injected into the non-addicted of their species are not to be lightly ignored, and should be matters of common scientific knowledge. The manifestations of addiction-disease in the new-born developed in the infant's body prenatally long before vice or habit or appetite can be possibly considered as causative factors, demand more than casual consideration and have a significance much deeper than as occasional curiosities.

An educational campaign as to the facts of addiction would save many an innocent person from the contraction of the disease, and many a present sufferer from unintelligent handling. Authoritative bodies with sufficient power and independence might easily institute unbiased review of what is written, and trial and proving out of what is stated by various writers, and give out their findings for the guidance of future work and action. Hospitals and public institutions for the handling of narcotic addicts may be erected Without comprehension of addiction-disease and full and complete familiarity with its manifestations, the possession of those who work in them, will they accomplish anything of good ?

The deduction from the testimony of the Whitney Investigation and from other sources leads to the conclusion that one of the reasons why the narcotic addict does not go to many of our present institutions is that he is more afraid of them, and anticipates more suffering in them than he cares to face in view of the fact that neither from previous personal experience or from repute he has little hope of being discharged from them in a condition of physical competency with his addiction mechanism arrested. He sees no use in going through them only to come out in a condition where he will have to revert to his opiate to enable him to endure and work. This is not an all-inclusive statement. It expresses, however, the frequent response of the addict seeking advice when asked why he does not go to the municipal institutions for treatment. Again then the work of those in the institutions will be the determining factor in their success or failure, and their education is the dominant element required for success. Some interesting observations upon this point will be found in the Yearly Report for the Department of Correction of New York City, 1915.

Of public clinics the same thing may be said. Whether they react to the benefit of the addict and of the community, or to the harm of the addict and community will depend upon their intelligent understanding and competent management.

Hospitals and clinics might be made into sorely needed educational centers for the training of doctors and nurses to go out and take up the work of the care of the addict — either private or institutional.

Education is the great need of the hour. Until it is accomplished all else will fail. Until we all know what we are dealing with, how can we hope to successfully handle it? It is to be hoped that the time is not far distant when in every medical school and hospital will be taught in principle and practice, in class-room and clinic all that is known or will be known of the pathology, symptomatology, physical phenomena and rational therapeutics of narcotic addiction-disease. It is to be hoped that in school and college, in pulpit and press, the facts of addiction will be presented in their practical existence, stripped of spectacularity; a calm, cold presentation of basic facts. There is no subject upon which philanthropy can better expend its forces than to this end of education as to addiction-disease and humane help to its sufferer.

In the past the problem of control of addiction has been " What shall be done *with* or what shall be done *to* the narcotic addict to make him stop using drugs? " It is now gradually coming to be realized that the true problem is " What can be done *for* the narcotic addict to relieve him of the physical necessity of using drugs? " and " What can be done to so educate the public as to the facts of addiction, so that this disease will claim as few victims as possible? "

In this change of attitude lies the hope for the future. Some of the narcotic addicts will have to be done *with* or done *to*. They are the inherently irresponsible, vicious or defective. They demand care and restraint irrespective of their addiction. The mass of addicts, however, need something done *for* them. They are clinical problems of internal medicine, victims of a definite disease, characteristic in its symptomatology, reactions and phenomena, a disease which will before long come to be known as clinically and therapeutically controllable and arrestable.

APPENDIX

HUMAN DOCUMENTS — PERSONAL STATEMENTS

The great importance of the real story of the sufferer from narcotic drug addiction-disease has been referred to several times in this book. It had been my first intention to include in the course of the various discussions, stories and statements of narcotic drug addicts illustrative of the various matters discussed, and to take them from my own collection of addiction histories.

That I might avoid any personal controversy, however, as to their personality or reliability, and also to make such statements free from any possible hint of influence or bias, I have taken them from medical literature and am using them as an appendix.

In December, 1917, *American Medicine* published a special addiction number, containing statements written for it by addicts of evident and vouched for intelligence and standing, stating their personal experiences and personal views.

Through the courtesy of *American Medicine* and its editors, I am reproducing these, believing that they are of great value and that they illustrate many of the discussions which appear in this book.

HUMAN DOCUMENTS [1]

THE PERSONAL SIDE OF DRUG ADDICTION

SOME VIEWS ON DRUG ADDICTION — PERSONAL AND LEGAL

BY A PROMINENT MEMBER OF THE NEW YORK BAR

A half dozen years ago I had a long, severe attack of gall-

[1] For obvious reasons the names of the authors of these contributions are not given. The editor, however, has every one of them, and has taken especial care to establish the authenticity and good faith of each article. Each contribution appears as received.

stones and inflammation of the gall-bladder. I suffered so much pain that the physicians gave me morphine for nearly a year. When I got better I tried my very best to get along without the drug, but could not. I came to a physician in New York for treatment who had made a special study of drug addiction and is a recognized authority on that subject. However, he could not help me at that time on account of a recurrence of my gall-bladder inflammation with severe jaundice and fever.

Since that time I have tried repeatedly to stop and reduce the quantity of the drug, but have found it impossible because of the physical pain and exhaustion due to the lack of the drug. This is unbearable. I have since then kept my daily amount of morphine medication at a minimum which permitted me to work and to maintain good health and bodily function. The idea which I have heard so often expressed, that addicts tend to increase their daily intake of narcotic, is certainly untrue in my case, and there seems to me no reason nor temptation to do so. I have simply found the smallest amount which would keep me from physical suffering, and have experienced no difficulty in maintaining that dosage, except in occasional emergencies of gall-bladder attacks or other crises, after which I found it a simple matter to discontinue the excess dosage. As I have never experienced the slightest pleasurable or sensually enjoyable sensations from the administration of morphine, there seems to me no foundation for this prevalent idea of tendency to increase. It may be true of the degenerate who has become addicted, but it certainly is untrue in my case, and must be untrue of the thousands like me whose misfortune it has been to become afflicted with this condition.

Recently I have again consulted specialists, and it seems that with my condition I must continue the administration of morphine for the present, and perhaps for the rest of my life. Physical conditions render present attempts to discontinue its use impractical, undesirable and dangerous.

Now what am I to do under the present "Drug Habit" laws of this State? I am a lawyer long past middle age — have held important state and judicial positions, and many positions of responsibility and trust. It would be ruinous to me if my addiction condition became public.

This law was enacted to control the drug traffic and to stop the evils which are connected with it. In many respects it is an excellent law, but the provisions which require the record of the name, age and residence of the addict to be filed in the Board of Health Office is outrageous. It does not affect the underworld, for they don't care and avoid registration by not going to those who have to register them. But see the position of a man who has a good reputation and standing in the community — forever recorded in the records of the State Board of Health as a " dope fiend," even though his condition is not the result of his own acts or desires and absolutely beyond his control.

This part of the law which requires the recording of the name, age and residence of the addict should be repealed. The only effect of these provisions is to record the addict as what everybody considers a " dope fiend " or force him to go to the smugglers for his drug. He must either place his good name and social and economic position in constant jeopardy or in some way or some way evade the law with its attendant penalty, and constant fear of detection. I should not be surprised if it finally develops to be the fact that a majority of decent sufferers from this condition have chosen the latter course as the lesser of evils.

I am informed that the Health Department has recently issued monthly registration blanks to physicians, demanding, in addition to the name, age and residence of the addict, the date and amounts of each prescription together with other information as to the individual cases treated. This makes conditions still more obnoxious and unbearable. Furthermore, this action of the authorities of the Board of Health is unwarranted and illegal. There is nothing in the powers of the Board of Health which permits them such action, and such action is without any justification in the letter of the law or in any possible interpretation of the spirit and intent of the law.

The data demanded were submitted to the Legislature as provisions in the law when the bill was being considered, and were rejected. The Health Department is usurping the powers of the Legislature, which it has no authority to do. The law plainly states what the physician shall report and the Board of Health has no power to require additional matters. Such action constitutes illegal interference with the rights of physician and patient as to matters of treatment and as to violation of professional confidence. It is my opinion that a narcotic addict might have grounds for legal procedure against a physician who furnished such information as the Health Department demands.

Conditions in New York today, affecting the honest addict, constitute in effect persecution of the sick. It is bad enough to be afflicted with this disease. Agonizing as gall-stone attacks have been, the physical suffering from lack of morphine in an addict is worse. Added to this is the knowledge that your name is on file at Albany, and perhaps elsewhere, as an addict. You know that disclosure of your condition will ruin you and disgrace your family. You are potentially subject to leakage from those records and the attendant possibilities of blackmail and other persecution. Such conditions tend to force and undoubtedly have forced many innocent and honest addicts of good social and economic standing to become criminals by obtaining their necessary opiate medicine through illegal channels.

Something certainly should be done to remedy existing conditions and existing laws. The great State of New York should not place its unfortunate sick in their present position.

THE PERSONAL HISTORY OF A MEDICAL ADDICT

BY A WELL-KNOWN AMERICAN PHYSICIAN

When the suggestion was first made by a medical friend that I should write a short account of my personal experience as a drug addict, particularly in reference to my status as a practitioner of medicine, the idea, for obvious reasons, was repellent, notwithstanding the fact that my identity should not be disclosed. But after mature deliberation, I realized that it is largely due to this natural reticence on the part of those in position to speak, that the unfortunate addict is regarded as a social pariah by the general public, and that until the medical profession shall acquire more accurate and less distorted knowledge of this serious question, we cannot hope for any improvement along these lines. Until this is done, cruel and unjust laws will be enforced, wretched victims will be imprisoned as felons, and what is more distressing, these unfortunates will, in many instances, be subjected to torture to which death is preferable — and not infrequently results. All this is based upon the accepted theory that drug addiction is a vicious habit requiring only a little fortitude and strength of will on the part of the wretched victim to rid himself of it, while the saddest feature of it all is that this canker, eating at the very heart of the nation itself, blighting and destroying the lives of many useful men and women, is not being reached.

That the average medical men can remain so hopelessly, I might say criminally, negligent of the true conditions of drug addiction is a cause for wonder as well as condemnation. If the perusal of my paper induces even one conscientious physician to seek more definite information upon this tremendously vital subject, my efforts shall not have been in vain. And now for my story.

At the age of 24 I had finished my medical and hospital courses and was ready to begin my career. My plans had long been formed with reference to entering the army as a surgeon; the decision having been made for two reasons, first as a matter of predilection; secondly, for lack of means to sustain me during the time usually required to establish a private practice.

Then a tragedy occurred that blasted my hopes for the army and altered my entire future.

The examinations were scheduled for the late spring; in January I had come down from my home in New England to New York to complete some clinical work. Generally, I was in bad shape, and about that time I began having attacks very suspicious of angina pectoris. Finally I consulted a great specialist, who after thorough and repeated examinations, frankly told me that from overwork and long hours of study my heart had become enlarged and badly disordered functionally — that I need never hope to pass the physical examination required for entrance to the army. He prescribed rest and freedom from care — two remedies entirely beyond my reach.

It was then that I went to a far distant city in the West to begin my career on a small amount of borrowed capital. It would be useless to dwell upon my struggles, hampered as I was by lack of funds and ill health, but in due time I became established. During the first few years my heart attacks were infrequent, but as work increased they returned, especially after an attack of typhoid fever which left my heart in a most disturbed state. Naturally, all· remedies were tried with an occasional rest, but to no avail. One night after a very trying day I was called to an obstetrical case; while hurriedly dressing I felt the premonitory symptoms of a heart attack; it was then in a state of desperation I took my first hypodermic. The attack was aborted, but the next day I was desperately sick. I may here add that at no time did I ever experience any of the ecstatic sensations described by some from a dose of morphine — it steadied my heart, but for some time after it was followed by a general malaise.

My obstetrical work increased rapidly and I frequently found it necessary to resort to the one remedy that proved efficacious. As was natural the time came when I found that the daily necessity had become fixed.

Having been taught that it was only a habit that required self will and force of character to abandon — both of which I knew I possessed — I was not particularly worried, as I had planned a long vacation when summer came, which I would devote to the accomplishment of my purpose. But for certain unavoidable reasons the vacation became impossible, and the next winter found me with added responsibilities.

During all this time I had constantly struggled against the increase of the drug. If under great pressure I was obliged to take an additional amount, as soon as it was over I began to reduce. There were occasions when I succeeded in taking only a fraction of my accustomed dose, but if a call came, I was either obliged to refuse it, or resort to the needle.

While naturally I had taken no one into my confidence, the habit had been so insidious and gradual that I had failed to realize how necessary it was that it should not be suspected. I did not consider myself an addict and only awaited a propitious occasion to relieve myself of it, but that winter I awoke to the realization that some radical step must be taken or my professional reputation would be damaged.

In the midst of this perplexity I developed an attack of la grippe and judging from past experience I felt that I would be confined to the house for some time, so resolved to take advantage of the enforced rest and abandon the use of the drug.

It was a hazardous and probably unwise decision, but I reasoned it was for the best. At the end of three weeks, after days and nights of physical and mental torture, I was able to leave my bed, freed from the specter that had haunted me, but for the time a wretched type of humanity. Four weeks of rest in the country enabled me to return to my practice, and although the heart attacks mercifully remained in abeyance, it was only by sheer force of will that I could accomplish my routine work, resting every spare moment that was afforded me, often refusing calls.

At the end of six months my work had so increased that the heart symptoms began to trouble me. The situation was desperate. Besides a wife and two children depending upon me I had other obligations, and was still in debt from my illness. I was unfitted for any other form of business.

I shall not enter into a discussion of the ethics of my act, but after sleepless nights of deliberation I reached the decision to return to the remedy that alone would enable me to attend to my duties, knowing all that it involved, but hoping that by constant vigilance to lessen the baneful effects of the drug until some day when I should be free to leave off work and again be cured.

During the years that followed, this object was ever before me, always fighting against an increase, devoting my vacations always to the same cause. In a measure I succeeded. I never progressed to extremely large doses, and I watched for and combatted any possible symptoms of peculiarity or degeneration that are supposed to obtain with the addict. I felt no sense of moral inferiority or degradation, nor did I deplete my strength with useless anticipation of dreaded possibilities. I would do all that lay in my power to preserve myself and the future lay in the hands of fate.

During these years success came to me. My clientele grew both in size and character. Positions of trust were conferred upon me, such as the examinership for some of the most important insurance companies, presidency of the County Medical Society, etc. I was elected visiting physician to two of our largest hospitals, and for some years did special work for the federal government, the nature of which for obvious reasons I do not care to mention.

In mentioning these facts, I do so with no vainglorious idea of boasting, but simply to record the history of my career. At the same time I used sometimes to ponder over the anomaly of my position — realizing with what horrified promptness the public would strip me of my honors, and transform its patronage and good will to contempt and pity, if it suspected the truth, although from its continued patronage my work was evidently entirely satisfactory. Even my intimate friends would shrink from me if the truth were known. Yet my philosophy and natural optimism sustained me.

It was at the end of about fifteen years that my circumstances were such that I felt in position to leave off work and take the long anticipated "cure." The institution selected was one whose methods seemed most reasonable. I stated to the specialist that I was anxious to be cured as rapidly as possible, and was willing to undergo whatever was necessary, to the limit of my endurance.

The three weeks that followed I remember as a horrid nightmare of mental and physical agony. The method was not intended to be harsh, and the physician was well-intentioned, though far from scientific.

In my desire for rapid recovery I overestimated my powers of endurance and my nervous system sustained a shock from which it has never recovered, but I persisted, with the assistance of my wife who remained with me and without whose assistance I should have lost my reason.

When I left the sanitarium I was no longer an " addict," but a wretched neurasthenic. Naturally the possibility of returning to my practice in this condition was not to be thought of so I began making plans to spend the winter in southern California. Here again the fates interposed. It was the autumn when the sudden financial panic swept the country, wrecking the fortunes of so many and tying up the resources of so many others. I was among the latter. There was nothing for me to do but to return to practice which I did after a further rest of six weeks — I need not add that in a short time I was again depending upon the drug to sustain me in the work that I was obliged to resume.

During the next five years I directed every energy towards shaping my affairs with the one end in view — that of retiring from practice and getting permanently well. By this time my two sons had finished their education and were established. My income was sufficient to provide us with the comforts, if not the luxuries of life. So with a heavy heart, but with a feeling of gratification, I abandoned the practice that I had acquired and sustained through so many years of bitter and sometimes heart-rending struggles.

My hopes for speedy restoration were doomed to disappointment. I should have realized that when release suddenly came from the long years of daily combat with so powerful an antagonist, a decided reaction must be the natural sequence. It came in the form of an almost complete prostration, that only by force of will prevented from permanently overcoming me; but more than two years elapsed before I felt equal to the effort of again submitting myself to treatment.

This time I selected a well-known specialist in the Middle West. I bared my entire life to his scrutiny, placing myself absolutely in his hands. Forty-eight hours as an inmate of the institution convinced me that I had made an unfortunate selection; but from a sense of false pride at being a " quitter " and a belief in my own powers I remained. The methods were absolutely crude and unscientific, the food poor and unsuitable, and the entire environment unfitted to the well being of such patients as I was.

At the end of seven weeks I was visited by the one most interested in me, who took me from my bed, from which I could not have arisen without assistance, and brought me

East. It is true that the amount of the drug that I had been taking had been reduced to a very small amount, but at the expense of a badly shattered nervous system which required many months to regain even its partial normal status.

This fall I am in New York and have placed myself under the care of a physician who, while not claiming to be a specialist has, in my opinion and the opinion of many others, the clearest conception of the meaning of drug addiction and its pathology. His opportunities for the study of these cases have been most unusual. His methods are both humane and scientific. Through him I have the hope that should time be allowed me I shall when I am summoned to the great unknown, be freed from the chains that so long oppressed but failed in the end to overwhelm me and compass my ruin.

DRUG ADDICTION FROM THE VIEWPOINT OF AN AFFLICTED PHYSICIAN

BY A PROMINENT MEDICAL MAN, FORMERLY A HEALTH OFFICIAL OF AN AMERICAN CITY

Maximum efficiency of every individual member of this nation is necessary today as never before in its history. Hence any condition responsible for lessened efficiency on the part of thousands of citizens is a thing to be seriously considered, especially when among these are to be found a large proportion of men and women who would otherwise be useful workers in every important field of activity.

Addiction to narcotic drugs is today depriving the country, either wholly or partially, of the services of thousands of individuals who but for this handicap would be entirely fit (many of them preeminently so) for work of the utmost importance. This is a problem of the first magnitude and one which will have to be solved largely by the medical profession.

But the medical profession as a whole is utterly lacking at the present time in such knowledge of addiction as is needed to enable them to attack the problem. For these reasons I feel it to be my duty to do my "bit" as a medical man, to put on record some of the lessons which, from years of personal experience, I have learned as to addiction itself, and the methods of treatment with which I have had experience in my efforts to be cured.

The subject is too important to excuse anything but the utmost frankness in speaking of the serious misconception which medical men only too generally share with the masses in regard to the subject of addiction. Unless the profession realizes its own ignorance, all point will be taken from the appeal which I wish to make to the physicians of this country to lose no time in equipping themselves to deal adequately with this great problem.

It may well be imagined that the task which I have thus set myself is no easy one, viewed from any one of half a dozen angles. Yet, if I am correct, in believing that I can thereby make a small contribution to the cause which now means so much to all of us, I must do so regardless of every difficulty.

Addiction with me goes back a number of years, covering in fact, almost my entire career as a physician. During this entire time, as will be more fully referred to, I have tried cure after cure, besides having, time and again, sought by own efforts to rid myself of this burden. I have naturally during these years studied and thought much about the problem which has meant so much to me. All this by way of showing why I believe that my experiences and opinions should have some value.

First of all, let it be clearly understood that the addiction which I shall discuss is limited strictly to opium and its derivatives; first, because my own experience is limited to this group and, second, because much that I shall have to say does not apply to all so-called habit-forming drugs to an equal extent, and to some of them not at all. Addiction as thus limited is as true a disease as any with which the human body is afflicted.

To look on the opium addict as a man with a vicious habit which he could quit if only he truly cared to do so displays a profound misunderstanding of plain facts. As well claim that a man with typical malarial infection has simply become so accustomed to having chills and fever at a given hour on certain days that when this hour arrives he quakes through mere habit as to claim that the equally characteristic and even more pronounced and distressing symptoms which manifest themselves when the addict is deprived of his drug are due to habit, that is, to " a condition which by repetition has become spontaneous."

We would, as a matter of fact, be less absurd in the former instance than in the latter; for we could argue the case out with our malarial friend, telling him he could conquer his "habit" by the exercise of will power, and — provided we argued long enough — we might convince ourselves that we were right because he would cease to shake, his fever would subside and until the next crop of parasites was turned loose in his blood stream, he would to all intents and purposes feel a well man, while in the latter case the more we talked of habit — that is, the longer the addict was deprived of his dose — the plainer would become the picture of a disease-racked body and a tormented mind.

I do not, of course, mean to offer the above comparison as either perfect in itself, or as sufficient to establish the claim that addiction is a true disease. The fact that it is a disease has impressed itself on all competent observers of a sufficient number of cases, and must be accepted. Yet it is astonishing to find that many educated physicians do not know this, while an even larger number, though readily admitting that addiction is a disease, nevertheless show, both by their manner of discussing the subject and by their attitude towards addicts seeking their advice, that this is little more than a verbal concession on their part.

If, however, it be argued that the contention as to addiction being a disease is vitiated by the fact that an occasional addict stops taking his drug by " will power," that is, without taking treatment, we can point to an even larger proportion of mild cases of malarial fever in which spontaneous cure has come about. But this does not prove that the one, any more than the other, is not a disease.

Indeed, there could be no stronger argument in favor of the fact that addiction is an actual disease than the very phenomena presented by the occasional addict who stops taking the drug by " will power." Neither medical writers nor literary geniuses, whether themselves addicts or mere observers, have yet succeeded in presenting a true picture of the tortures which this involves. There could be no greater error than to regard cure as dating from the time the last dose was taken. When, in these cases, cure comes at all, it is only after weeks, or months, of horrible existence, during which kind nature brings about a more or less complete restoration of body and mind not alone from the disease of addiction, but also from the profound shock of unskilled or unwise withdrawal. Will power has enabled the addict to abstain from taking the drug, while nature cured the disease.

There has been no time during all the years of my addiction that I have not earnestly longed to be free from its clutches. This is sufficiently proved by the many efforts which I have made to find a cure, each time at great personal sacrifice and expense, each time only to have my hopes shattered, after untold suffering and fresh disillusionment.

But a real cure I have thus far been unable to find. I have tried everything that seemed to offer a chance: gradual reduction, self-conducted and at institutions, the Keeley cure several times, and since then all of the vaunted cures, as each appeared in turn, advocated by men of high standing in the medical profession. Concerning this last class, I have each time hoped that such men could not be totally in error as to the practical results of their methods, notwithstanding what has seemed to me the most bizarre pathology on which they have claimed these methods to be based.

I might, perhaps, have been warned by certain palpable danger signs, but I have been too anxious to find the cure. I cared not at all how mistaken their pathology; for I could not believe that men of such standing could be equally mistaken as to the success or failure of what went on under their very eyes.

And right here let me set down what has impressed me as inexcusable neglect of these cases by most of these self same " big " men of the medical profession. One after another I have found physicians who receive and undertake to treat cases of addiction brought to them by the lure of high professional reputation and medical articles in which is painted a glowing picture of some new and wonderful cure. And, one after another, I have found these men of high professional standing giving to their cases not even enough time and attention to enable them to form an intelligent opinion as to their condition and progress, much less what would be needed for the proper study and treatment of one of the most difficult and distressing ailments which afflict mankind.

Moreover, comparing notes with medical men who have been fellow patients under similar circumstances (many of them, I may remark, of the highest type, as men and as physicians), there has been among us a universal sense of shame and indignation that men with such reputation and standing should lay the medical profession open to the justly founded criticism of extortion and neglect of duty, frequently of seemingly rank commercialism, even including the splitting of fees with quacks and charlatans of the worst sort.

In saying that I have found no cure, I do not mean that I have never succeeded in getting to the point where I could get along for shorter or longer periods without the drug. Many times I have succeeded by myself in gradually reducing the dose to a minimum and then making the final plunge and taking none at all for some time. What this has meant I will not undertake to describe. Several times I have managed to keep from using the drug for a while after taking treatment of one kind or another. But have I been cured?

Let no one thoughtlessly reply that the very fact of my having on each of these occasions reached a point where, according to my own statement, I was able to live without the drug, constitutes proof that I was cured, or that when I started to use it again I was merely yielding weakly.

What has actually happened has been this. Each time that I have succeeded, in one way or another, in reaching a point where I was no longer taking the drug, I have, even while the suffering was still acute, been filled with a sense of happiness and hope that enabled me to stand it thankfully. I have argued with myself that, being then able even to exist without the drug and, for a while finding this existence day by day a little less of torture, I might reasonably hope for continued improvement. I have not expected miracles, but I have felt that each week should be easier, until, after a period of some few months, I should again be normal.

But this has not come about. Always I have reached a point where progress seemed to stop, and beyond this point my system refused to react. Occasionally this standstill has been quickly reached, that is, I could not react beyond a point where I was unable to sleep, where my legs ached atrociously, and where I was so completely unstrung that life was unendurable. At best, progress has continued for a few weeks, after which, though resting well, having a prodigious appetite and not undergoing marked physical suffering, I have actually been far from normal. This was shown, on these special occasions, chiefly by my inability to do satisfactory work, by my tiring altogether too easily and by a general feeling of unrest and disquietude.

I realize the difficulty of so describing my condition during these most favorable occasions as to show at all convincingly that I was not actually cured and that, in consequence, my resuming the taking of the drug was anything but a relapse. This, however, I must not attempt to do, since the main contention which I wish to make is here directly led up to.

And, hard as is the whole task I have set myself in writing this account, this special part of it is peculiarly difficult, involving the risk of appearing to set a false value on certain personal considerations.

My life has been an active and useful one. I have done work which I know to be good and which has brought recognition. Successful work, even in a given line of endeavor, is not always due to the same qualities in different men. My own work has been characterized by the exercise of careful judgment and the power of accurate analysis, qualities which I have always been credited with possessing. Now, after the most favorable of the so-called treatments which I have taken, and after allowing considerable time for complete recovery, I have in no instance regained these most essential requisites for my work, and thus I have been placed in a position where I would either have had to discontinue my work, or else do the only thing which made the resuming of that work possible. And always there has been the absolute conviction that this state of affairs was due to my not having been actually cured. On this point there has not been one iota of doubt.

Perhaps if I had been able at such times to take a complete rest of six months or even a year, I might have been fully restored, but this has not been possible. I have not been able to remain away from work for over five or six weeks after the "cure" proper, and even this has, as may well be understood, been a severe drain, when I have taken some cure or other at as short intervals as I could manage to get together sufficient funds and the opportunity to leave my practice.

Of course it may be argued that, rather than return to the use of the drug and thus again be able to live a life as nearly approaching normal as is possible for an addict, it would be better to refrain from using the drug, even though this involved never again being able to do those things which, to the ambitious man, are essential to make life worth the living. I submit that it is a high motive and not a low one which makes a man willing to pay the price rather than live a vegetative existence when he knows himself capable of better things. To understand this point of view it must be remembered that the addict gets no rosy dreams, no wonderful journeys into a beautiful and unreal world, no artificially enhanced powers beyond those of the non-addict, but at best only such equanimity and energy as are the latter's happy possessions.

My point, therefore, is that my resorting to the drug after having stopped its use a number of times does not mean that I have many times been cured, and many times relapsed, but that I have not been truly cured. When the latest "cure" which I have taken has left me, even after weeks, still suffering acutely and continuously, and not improving in the slightest so far as I could see, I have taken the drug again for relief from torture no longer bearable. After "cures" which have left me in decidedly better plight but in the intolerable condition last described above, and with progress at a standstill, I have taken the drug only after calmly surveying the situation, and as the lesser of two evils.

I must reiterate my strong desire to find a cure, a real cure, one deserving the name; that is, a cure which will leave me normal, without need of the drug, and able to do the work which I must do in the world unless I am willing to be a slacker. But until I can find such a cure (and, in spite of my unhappy experiences, I will keep up the quest) I would have only contempt for myself as a physician and as a rational being if I failed meanwhile to make the best compromise possible, namely, to take each day, just as I would take thyroid substance were I suffering from hypothyroidism, a sufficient amount of morphine to enable me to attend to life's duties and to occupy in the world that useful place which my qualifications enable me to occupy.

One of the great hardships under which every addict suffers is the constant dread lest his affliction become known and he be branded a "morphine fiend," a term which should be prohibited, or at least never used by an intelligent physician. What this exposure would mean to a man of standing in his community I need not explain. This risk he must always run, but it would be robbed of some of its terror if the nature of addiction were better understood.

Therefore the law now existing in some states requiring the registration of addicts is little short of barbarous. So little possible good can be accomplished by this law that one is tempted to believe that its passage was not instigated primarily by honest, though misguided zealots but by quite another class. The addict, in his efforts to find a cure, has learned something of a class of men, who, posing as public benefactors, are in reality a shrewd set of rascals, capitalizing the misfortunes of the addict most successfully. If such men were not the originators of the idea of registration, certainly they, and not the body politic, are its chief beneficiaries, since it affords them an authentic list of prospective victims.

As for the effect of this law on the addict, it merely adds further to his dread of exposure. Think of the position of a man of prominence and respected in his community, having his own feelings as have other men, holding equally dear the sensibilities of those he loves, living under the constant dread that his necessities may any day force him to seek aid in a state in which his name will, as it were, be added to a rogues' gallery!

My plea is for realization of the great need for finding some means whereby the individual addict may get real relief and whereby addicts collectively may be restored to such condition as will render them capable of performing those services of which our country is now in need.

I am confident that I am understating the case when I say that nine addicts out of ten earnestly desire to be cured. Why should they not? They get no pleasure out of taking the drug, but only relief from intolerable suffering which they must otherwise endure. Hence to be free both from this suffering and from the necessity of getting this relief by artificial, and at present exceedingly costly, means is bound to appeal to them. Most addicts, I am confident, are willing to go through whatever acute suffering may be involved in any really rational treatment which will, after a reasonable time, restore them to normal condition.

Experiences such as I have described above are, I know, the rule and not the exception with those who have tried the various so-called cures. They can hardly be called satisfactory. Even admitting that they may prove successful in a small proportion of cases, relatively few addicts are able to find the means of taking them, such as I have been able to make for myself in the midst of a very active life.

Surely a disease having so definite a symptomatology and, I believe, so plain a pathology, must be susceptible of rational cure. That such a cure has not yet been found by those who so loudly proclaim to have found one I honestly believe. Whether others have devised more promising lines of treatment I frankly do not know.

But a cure must be found which does more than any I have succeeded in finding. In what other disease would a patient who, after reaching a certain point, beyond which he could not progress towards recovery, be told that from then on everything rested with him, although he himself knew that his need for help was really as great as it ever was? In what other disease would any physician worthy of the name calmly tell a patient that, having taken a " cure," he was, *ipse facto,* cured, and become highly incensed when the patient pleaded that his condition was in many respects more desperate than before treatment?

The medical profession must seriously study addiction. Of material there is, unfortunately, an abundance. Some high authority should see that every facility is afforded the proper persons for employing it. It is not unlikely that many of the " cures " which have been advocated have in them some elements of good, properly selected and properly applied in each individual case. Possibly competent investigation, furnished with every facility, might result in the discovery of a truly specific cure. I have long thought that there was such a possibility in more than one direction, but investigation of these would involve very careful and laborious work, as well as considerable cost. Here indeed, would seem to be a wonderful opportunity for philanthropy.

But while such a specific cure would be an untold blessing, we need not find one in order to meet the situation — at least, much more successfully than it is being met at present. Coordination of the entire problem of addiction, in the hands of the few men whose work in this field is most promising (and the men I have in mind are not those with whose vaunted cures I have had such unhappy experiences) would almost certainly lead to valuable results.

While every effort should be exerted to determine the best lines of treatment, meanwhile there is a great deal which should be done in other directions. Let the medical profession help in bringing about better understanding of addiction — first, of course, learning this themselves. Until the addict can be offered rational treatment, the profession should do what it can in making the lives of addicts less unbearable by removing from the public mind some of the gross misconceptions concerning addiction, seeing to it, especially, that these unfortunates are not stigmatized as " morphine fiends " and that they are given the means of obtaining, without risk and hardship and almost prohibitive cost, the supply of their drug which, until they are cured, is to them as necessary as the air they breathe.

But the finding of a real cure or treatment — not necessarily specific, not a thing to be applied indiscriminately in every case, but a rational method of handling addiction as other well known diseases are handled — is the great aim, or, if it be that sufficient is already known by some men in the profession as to the rational handling of addicts, let these men be found and their services subsidized by the government and used to the fullest extent, in teaching others, and these still others, until there is built up a system extending over the entire country, capable and equipped for giving to every addict the opportunity for cure. This is a crying need in our country today. Surely there must be somewhere recognition of this fact and resources enough to make it possible for this need to be supplied.

A Plea for the Broader Consideration of Narcotic Drug Addiction by the Medical Profession

By a Practicing Physician Who Has Met the Problem in His Own Family

In view of a recent experience of mine in seeking intelligent medical help for a near relative whom I learned was a narcotic drug addict, I take pleasure in recounting experiences of the past few months in the handling of such a case, and in calling attention to the conditions which my investigations have shown me to exist in our profession.

My line of professional activity had not brought me knowingly into touch with narcotic drug addiction, and I entertained the prevailing medical opinions in regard to it.

About five months ago I received a letter couched in apologetic language from a practitioner in another state informing me that a younger brother of mine had been under his care for a number of days suffering from withdrawal symptoms occasioned by inability to purchase morphine, and advising me to place him in some institution where he could be restrained.

I immediately began asking my colleagues where I could send such a case, and was amazed at the general lack of knowledge in regard to and sympathy for these unfortunates. In truth no one could point out a single institution where such a patient could be sent with any hope that he might be handled in a humane and intelligent manner.

My investigations of the institutions they suggested showed this to be the fact.

Most every one seems to regard those suffering from this condition as being of a lower order of humanity, unwilling or too weak-minded to help themselves and fit subjects only for association with what is commonly known as the " underworld." I wish to say that I myself have undergone a very complete revision of mind regarding these cases since the case of my brother has compelled me to investigate them. I have known my brother too well and for too many years to believe that he can possibly be placed in any such category.

I have made careful inquiries into the circumstances and origin of his addiction, and the results are absolutely convincing that the first administrations of the narcotic were to meet therapeutic indications and were continued without his knowledge or appreciation of its actions or ultimate results. I know that he has never experienced any pleasure from the narcotic, and I know that when the condition of addiction manifested itself he did not know what was the matter with him. He only knew that narcotic relieved intense suffering. I had never seen a case of addiction to my knowledge before I went to see him in response to the letter I received. The clinical symptomatology of withdrawal of an opiate was truly a revelation to me. That the condition from which these patients suffer is a distinct disease cannot be questioned by any intelligent observer.

I have found that the majority of patients who begin the use of opiates do so in search of relief from pain, and are not aware of the fact for a long time that the suffering they endure when the drug is discontinued is due to a disease they have contracted. Apparently the medical profession is also ignorant of this fact.

A more pathetic sight I have never seen than one of these patients who has been suddenly deprived of his medicine. They will tell you that they will become insane or be driven to suicide if they cannot obtain relief from their suffering. Hence their willingness to obtain the drug at any cost. I have come to believe that any man is justifiable in lying or stealing to escape the agonies I have witnessed.

It seems a crime that we of the profession have gone so long without any attempt to study or understand the disease which we in our daily rounds are constantly creating. Certainly our standard medical literature contains little if anything of value in regard to this condition, and investigation of the claims and procedure of the widely advertised so-called "treatments" and "cures" readily convinces one of their unworthiness.

I know that much can be done for the cure of these patients by an intelligent effort on the part of the medical profession, and a willingness to open their minds to the clinical facts of this condition and to handle it like other diseases.

In search of information I have gotten into touch with cases of addiction other than my brother's, and I find that the majority of them are desperately anxious to be cured. They tell me, however, that institutions such as jails, workhouses, lunatic asylums, alcoholic wards of the charity hospitals, and those that they have tried of the advertised cures are places of insufferable torture from which they emerge in worse condition than that in which they entered.

There are estimated to be as many as 500,000 or more addiction cases in the State of New York alone. I ask in all earnestness, is it not worth while to try to do something more than we are doing for these sufferers?

PRINTED IN THE UNITED STATES OF AMERICA

INDEX

INDEX

PRINTED IN THE UNITED STATES OF AMERICA

SOCIAL PROBLEMS
AND
SOCIAL POLICY:
The American Experience

An Arno Press Collection

Bachman, George W. and Lewis Meriam. **The Issue of Compulsory Health Insurance.** 1948

Bishop, Ernest S. **The Narcotic Drug Problem.** 1920

Bosworth, Louise Marion. **The Living Wage of Women Workers.** 1911

[Brace, Emma, editor]. **The Life of Charles Loring Brace.** 1894

Brown, Esther Lucile. **Social Work as a Profession.** 4th Edition. 1942

Brown, Roy M. **Public Poor Relief in North Carolina.** 1928

Browning, Grace. **Rural Public Welfare.** 1941

Bruce, Isabel Campbell and Edith Eickhoff. **The Michigan Poor Law.** 1936

Burns, Eveline M. **Social Security and Public Policy.** 1956

Cahn, Frances and Valeska Bary. **Welfare Activities of Federal, State, and Local Governments in California, 1850-1934.** 1936

Campbell, Persia. **The Consumer Interest.** 1949

Davies, Stanley Powell. **Social Control of the Mentally Deficient.** 1930

Devine, Edward T. **The Spirit of Social Work.** 1911

Douglas, Paul H. and Aaron Director. **The Problem of Unemployment.** 1931

Eaton, Allen in Collaboration with Shelby M. Harrison. **A Bibliography of Social Surveys.** 1930

Epstein, Abraham. **The Challenge of the Aged.** 1928

Falk, I[sidore] S., Margaret C. Klem, and Nathan Sinai. **The Incidence of Illness and the Receipt and Costs of Medical Care Among Representative Families.** 1933

Fisher, Irving. **National Vitality, its Wastes and Conservation.** 1909

Freund, Ernst. **The Police Power:** Public Policy and Constitutional Rights. 1904

Gladden, Washington. **Applied Christianity:** Moral Aspects of Social Questions. 1886

Hartley, Isaac Smithson, editor. **Memorial of Robert Milham Hartley.** 1882

Hollander, Jacob H. **The Abolition of Poverty.** 1914

Kane, H[arry] H[ubbell]. **Opium-Smoking in America and China.** 1882

Klebaner, Benjamin Joseph. **Public Poor Relief in America, 1790-1860.** 1951

Knapp, Samuel L. **The Life of Thomas Eddy.** 1834

Lawrence, Charles. **History of the Philadelphia Almshouses and Hospitals from the Beginning of the Eighteenth to the Ending of the Nineteenth Centuries.** 1905

[Massachusetts Commission on the Cost of Living]. **Report of the Commission on the Cost of Living.** 1910

[Massachusetts Commission on Old Age Pensions, Annuities and Insurance]. **Report of the Commission on Old Age Pensions, Annuities and Insurance.** 1910

[New York State Commission to Investigate Provision for the Mentally Deficient]. **Report of the State Commission to Investigate Provision for the Mentally Deficient.** 1915

[Parker, Florence E., Estelle M. Stewart, and Mary Conymgton, compilers]. **Care of Aged Persons in the United States.** 1929

Pollock, Horatio M., editor. **Family Care of Mental Patients.** 1936

Pollock, Horatio M. **Mental Disease and Social Welfare.** 1941

Powell, Aaron M., editor. **The National Purity Congress;** Its Papers, Addresses, Portraits. 1896

The President's Commission on the Health Needs of the Nation. **Building America's Health.** [1952]. Five vols. in two

Prostitution in America: Three Investigations, 1902-1914. 1975

Rubinow, I[saac] M. **The Quest for Security.** 1934

Shaffer, Alice, Mary Wysor Keefer, and Sophonisba P. Breckinridge. **The Indiana Poor Law.** 1936

Shattuck, Lemuel. **Report to the Committee of the City Council Appointed to Obtain the Census of Boston for the Year 1845.** 1846

The State and Public Welfare in Nineteenth-Century America: Five Investigations, 1833-1877. 1975

Stewart, Estelle M. **The Cost of American Almshouses.** 1925

Taylor, Graham. **Pioneering on Social Frontiers.** 1930

[United States Senate Committee on Education and Labor]. **Report of the Committee of the Senate Upon the Relations Between Labor and Capital.** 1885. Four vols.

Walton, Robert P. **Marihuana, America's New Drug Problem.** 1938

Williams, Edward Huntington. **Opiate Addiction.** 1922

Williams, Pierce assisted by Isabel C. Chamberlain. **The Purchase of Medical Care Through Fixed Periodic Payment.** 1932

Willoughby, W[estal] W[oodbury]. **Opium as an International Problem.** 1925

Wisner, Elizabeth. **Public Welfare Administration in Louisiana.** 1930

D TE DUE